A NEW ZIONISM

A NEW ZIONISM

by

MORDECAI M. KAPLAN

Second Enlarged Edition

Published by
THE HERZL PRESS
and the
JEWISH RECONSTRUCTIONIST PRESS
New York 1959

DS
149
K45
1969
cop. 3

PRINTED IN THE UNITED STATES OF AMERICA

BY H. GANTT, PUBLISHERS PRINTING REPRESENTATIVE

360 CABRINI BLVD., NEW YORK CITY 40, N. Y.

FOREWORD

THE MAIN MESSAGE OF THIS TRACT is that the Zionist movement is now faced with the choice of either folding up or
assuming the responsibility of reconstituting the Jewish People and giving it a new lease on life. This responsibility is
not unrelated to the establishment of the State of Israel, but,
on the contrary is the inevitable óutcome of that achievement
of Zionism. It has to be assumed, if the State is to weather
the many storms that lie ahead of it. Far from involving the
abandonment of any of the tasks that are still part of Zionism's unfinished business, the assumption of that responsibility
would guarantee the consummation of those tasks.

Fortunately, what is set forth in this tract is no longer
confined to the pages that follow. It has passed over to Zionist forums and periodicals. Its main recommendations formed
the content of the Proposed Platform reported at the 1958
Convention of the Zionist Organization of America by its
Special Commission on Zionist Ideology. From there that
Proposed Platform has passed over to the American Zionist
Council, a special committee of which is at present in the
process of hammering it out for presentation at the forthcoming convention of the World Zionist Organization. Simultaneously, steps are being taken to reorganize the Zionist
movement itself, which will facilitate the adoption and the
effective functioning of the Greater Zionism.

In view of the foregoing considerations, the republication
in enlarged form of this tract is altogether timely. It will help
to acquaint the general public with what is at stake in the
transition which has to take place from the Old Zionism to
the New Zionism, if the gains so far attained are to be retained and new ones to be acquired. If it is true, as is argued
in this tract, that the crisis in Zionism is the crisis in Judaism,
no self-respecting Jew can afford to ignore the issues presented
in this tract. He should study them carefully and give the
Jewish People the benefit of his most careful and conscientious
judgment.

MORDECAI M. KAPLAN

May, 1959

FOREWORD TO THE FIRST EDITION

I wish to express my indebtedness to The Jewish Agency and The Jewish Theological Seminary of America for having given me the opportunity, through the Seminary-Israel Institute, to formulate my views concerning the direction which the Zionist movement should now take. I am particularly grateful to Dr. Moshe Davis, who, in behalf of the Seminary-Israel Institute, not only invited me to give the 1954 Lecture Series but also talked me out of my reluctance to accept the invitation because of pressure of routine duties. My thanks also go to Dr. Ben Halpern for his challenging questions and helpful suggestions, and to Mr. Moshe Kohn for his careful editing of my manuscript.

Mordecai M. Kaplan

New York, January, 1955

The present volume is based on the course of six lectures delivered by Professor Kaplan *for the Seminary-Israel Institute, sponsored by* The Jewish Theological Seminary of America *and* The Jewish Agency for Palestine, *from February 16 to March 23, 1954.*

Chapter VII, newly added to this edition, is based on an address delivered at the convention of the Zionist Organization of America on October 24th, 1958.

CONTENTS

DEDICATED TO THE MEMORY OF

HAYIM GREENBERG

*who, devoted to the vision of a
Jewry eternally united, sponsored
the founding of the*
SEMINARY-ISRAEL INSTITUTE

CHAPTER I
The Crisis In Zionism
As Crisis In Judaism

I

ONE OF THE MAIN SOURCES of preventable evil is man's unpreparedness for the good fortune that comes his way. Because of his unpreparedness to derive the good from the opportunity offered him, that opportunity may even turn into a source of danger, to the extent, at times, of threatening his existence. Suffering and death are a result of man's premature use of the knowledge that gives him power. One might construct a philosophy of history based upon that thesis, and illustrate it with examples drawn from the career of every people, since the dawn of human history when man discovered the uses of fire, to the present day when he is in a dither because of his inability to master the inexhaustible power which he has learned to release from the atom.

One might likewise formulate on the basis of that thesis a philosophy of Jewish history, beginning with the Exodus from Egypt, which found our ancestors unprepared for entry into the Promised Land, down to our own day, when we Jews find ourselves unprepared as a people to avail ourselves fully of the opportunity presented us by the establishment of the State of Israel. A century and a half ago came the Jewish emancipation, and, with it, limitless opportunity to enlarge our horizons of human knowledge and endeavor. But we were caught frightfully unprepared. That accounts, in large part, for the heavy price we have been paying in the defection of our most talented and gifted men and women.

Now more than ever must we Jews lay to heart the teaching of Ahad Ha'am, the main point of which even his own followers seem to have missed. That point is that the only way in which

the return of Jews to Eretz Yisrael can come to mean the fulfillment of the long nurtured hope of the Jewish People, is for the
Jewish People to prepare itself for that fulfillment by undergoing
what is tantamount to a metamorphosis. Without a Jewish people
regenerated in spirit, no matter how successful the state that it
would establish, and how large a population that state could
muster, Zion will continue to be unredeemed.

Events have a way of their own. They have *compelled*
us Jews to establish a state. We have had to disregard Ahad
Ha'am's warning. However, the inevitable consequence against
which he warned us has come about. All hopes that the return
to Eretz Yisrael would spell the regeneration of the entire Jewish
People seem to have been postponed *sine die*.

But if we Jews will take a leaf out of our past, we should
be able to transcend this disillusionment, and try to make good
the lack of preparation which has brought it about. It is this
ability that has enabled us to come out alive, even if limping,
after many a struggle with angels of darkness and despair. It
is the purpose of this tract to suggest a New Zionism which
might serve as the preparation needed to render the upbuilding
of Eretz Yisrael an occasion for the regeneration of the Jewish
People.

A division of opinion which had been inherent in the Zionist
movement from its very inception has been sharpened by the
establishment of the State of Israel. It is the division of opinion
which took rise in the controversy between Herzl and Ahad
Ha'am. It turned upon the question of what should be the
immediate objective of the Zionist movement. Should it be the
acquisition of a legally assured home in Eretz Yisrael for the
Jewish People, as Herzl maintained? Or should it be the perpetuation of the Jewish People and its cultural heritage through
the renaissance of Jewish life in Eretz Yisrael, as Ahad Ha'am
would have it?

When, at the beginning of the century, after the death of
Herzl, the prospect of an immediate realization of his program
appeared remote, Ahad Ha'am's version of Zionism became the

order of the day. Zionists then took a leading part in consolidating the Jewish communities in the Diaspora, and in fostering a culturally enriched Hebraic education. Not long after Britain was granted the Palestine Mandate, Herzlian Zionism gained the upper hand in the United States, through the accession of new forces headed by Justice Louis D. Brandeis, and later through the creation of the Jewish Agency for Palestine in which non-Zionists were given representation.

At the present time, the issue over which Zionists are divided threatens to throw confusion into the Zionist movement, to jeopardize the State of Israel, and to disintegrate further the unity of the Jewish People. The issue is the *negation* of the Diaspora *vs.* the *affirmation* of the Diaspora. It is virtually the recrudescence, under more critical circumstances, and in a sharper form, of the controversy between Herzl and Ahad Ha'am. A resolution of that controversy is far more urgent now than it has ever been, because the State of Israel is now a living reality. *Unless Zionism can develop at once a basis for a strong sense of mutuality and interaction between the Jewish community in Israel and the Jewish communities in the rest of the world, something altogether different from what either Herzl or Ahad Ha'am envisaged is likely to emerge.*

It is regrettable that we have to resort to the analogy of a military campaign to illustrate what has to be done in conducting so humanitarian and idealistic a campaign as Zionism. Yet that is the simplest way of indicating what's wrong at the present time with the Zionist movement, and what is necessary to set it right.

From a tactical standpoint, Zionists seem, on the whole, to do the best that can be expected of them, though there is no telling what constitutes one's best. But the same cannot be said of their concern with the strategy of the movement. They seldom give thought to strategy, and if they do, some of their most noted leaders dismiss it as superfluous, if not troublesome. One such leader of American Zionism made it a point at the recent convention of the Zionist Organization of America to pooh-pooh all attempts to rethink the philosophy of Zionism. "What we need," he declared, "is not a new philosophy but a renewed dedication to the great cause to which we, by our efforts in the past, have contributed so much, but which is not fully consummated" (*The American Zionist,* July, 1954). In the light of the well-known definition of a fanatic as one who redoubles his effort when he loses his purpose, that sounds like a call to fanaticism.

What strategy is to a military campaign, a philosophy is to Zionism. The establishment of the State of Israel was, no doubt, a great tactical victory for Zionism. But has it been consolidated into a strategic victory? How can we tell, unless we know what the Zionist strategy really is? It was, indeed, good to hear what Rabbi Irving Miller had to say at the same convention about strategy. "The historic end of Zionism," he said, "remains the fulfillment of the cultural and spiritual values of our people. It remains in its basic significance the perpetuation of the Jewish people. It is, indeed, Jewish survival itself" (*Ib.*). But neither Rabbi Miller nor any one else at that convention found it necessary to ask how much the State of Israel is serving to bring Jews nearer to that goal.

In a military campaign there is always the danger of winning battles but losing the war, and even if the war is won, of losing the peace. Zionism faces a similar danger. It is altogether possible that every tactical battle on the Zionist front may be won, and yet the over-all purpose for which those battles should have been fought may be lost. It is even possible that the over-all purpose may be won *de jure,* but not *de facto.*

We cannot stress sufficiently the urgency of the *immediate* tasks that confront Israel. *The resettlement and development of the land and safeguarding its borders from hostile attacks cannot wait for the outcome of discussions of strategy.* They must be given priority over our other Jewish responsibilities and activities. But we dare not permit those immediate tasks to blur the larger Zionist perspective which takes in the whole of world Jewry. We must not omit from our reckoning the impact of the State of Israel on the will to Jewish survival. We should not ignore as irrelevant to Zionism the ominous reports that reach us from Israel, of trends which threaten to kill the hope that Judaism, as an evolving religious civilization, would experience a revival there. If those trends continue to make headway, that would certainly be the end of Zionism, and in all likelihood, also of Judaism.

If the State of Israel is to fulfill its Zionist mission, the problems of nationhood, religion and Diaspora will have to be dealt with by a permanent international Jewish conference created for that purpose, or by an existing institution like the Hebrew University, which should establish such a conference. That conference will have to disentangle the knottiest of human problems. But such is the desperate need of Jews in and outside Israel for some kind of workable solution which will give meaning and direction to their lives, that a way out of the present impasse must be found as soon as possible.

Zionism would experience a much needed self-renewal if, now that the fiscal problems of Israel have been largely taken over by other agencies, the Zionist Organization, in addition to serving as liaison agency between Israel and the non-Jewish world, sponsored the move for the establishment of such a conference.

II

The situation in Zionism is far from encouraging. The World Zionist movement is on the wane. The very need for the continuance of Zionism is being questioned, since, with the establishment of the State of Israel, its main purpose seems to have been achieved, and since most, if not all, of its functions either have been, or can be, taken over either by the State, or by pro-Israel agencies. Zionists, like the radicals of a generation ago, have become "tired." They are losing their zeal for Zionism.

As long as Zionism was merely a dream, it suffered none of the disheartenments which have come with its realization. Like a newborn infant, the State of Israel was no sooner born than it contracted all the possible diseases of an infant state. To cure those ills, Zionism has to enlarge its vision and to broaden the scope of its interests and activities.

From an economic and strategic standpoint, it is held that the survival of the State calls for a population of four million

within ten years. At present there are only 1,600,000, of whom
200,000 are Arabs. Where are the necessary 2,400,000 to come
from? It is futile to expect the countries behind the Iron Curtain
to open their doors. Nor can the Jews of the West, with pre-
State Zionism as the only motivation, be counted on to emigrate
to Israel.

The expectation at the beginning of the new State that the
new immigrants would follow the example set by the pioneers
who had laid the foundations of the country, has turned out to
be illusory. Among those who have entered the land as a result
of artificial stimulation from within or persecution from without, the abnormally large proportion of incapacitated dependents
has created a problem rather than an asset for the struggling
State. Nor are there enough vigorous, enterprising and pioneering
men and women to direct the process of absorbing the recent
immigrants and rendering them productive by giving them occu-
pational training. "Failing an adequate influx of settlers from
Western countries," we are told, "the entire edifice that has been
created is in danger of collapse" (Elizer Livneh, *State and Diaspora*, p. 67).

As long as the members of the Arab League maintain their
blockade and boycott, their hostile propaganda and unceasing
border attacks, and the Israeli Government has to depend upon
United States good-will and grants-in-aid, the State of Israel cannot escape a sense of continuing danger. Israel is besieged on
three sides by eight Arab states which are united by one purpose
of destroying her.

In the meantime, too, there has begun to emerge a new
bond of Islamic unity which may prove a threat not only to
Israel but to world peace. Early in August, 1954 the rulers of
Egypt, Pakistan and Saudi Arabia met in the sacred city of
Mecca to launch a missionary crusade with the avowed purpose
of saving Africa from Christianity and Communism, but with
the actual purpose of curbing the Western powers. That is all
the more reason why Israel must strengthen her ties with the
Western nations. But for her tie-up with the Western nations the
Jewish communities among them are an indispensable link.

*So long as the State is still in the process of being consoli-
dated, so long as it has to be rendered secure against onslaught
from without and weakness from within, Zionism is far from being
a finished business.* Far from slowing up the Zionist movement,
those dangers should normally impart new impetus to it. The
members of the first migration, the *Biluim,* in 1882, or of the
Second Aliya (migration), in 1904, had to cope with difficulties
which at the time could only appear insuperable. One need but
recall the suffering which the first World War brought on the
Jewish colonies. They suffered unemployment and hunger. The
Turkish government deported the most important leaders, jailed
many who were left, and cut them off from all contact with the
rest of the world. The present predicament of Zionism, on the
other hand, does not appear insurmountable. And there is every
reason in the world why American Jews should come to the
rescue. "A politically unstable, financially impoverished and culturally declining State of Israel," writes Livneh (*State and Diaspora,* p. 49), "would react to the detriment of American Jews,
including even non-Zionists." Why, then, is there a falling off in
Zionist membership, and why is United Jewish Appeal and Israel
Bond drive income steadily decreasing?

Even more disconcerting is the growing contempt for Zionism on the part of Jews in Israel. "If you ask the *sabra,* who has
no sentimental attachment to the past," writes Livneh, "what is
the Zionist movement? he will surely answer that it is a combination of futility, loquacity and duplication of effort. If you keep
asking him that same question, he will probably say: It is a number of people who make frequent trips to various countries. The
purpose of those trips is vague and their value is questionable
but since the entire business is not at our expense—let them go on
with it. . . . If you ask: Is there any need for the Zionist Organization to fulfill the functions in which it is engaged? you will
be answered with a shrug. . . . The Zionist agency is looked upon
by many as a philanthropic institution, reminiscent of the era of
halukah—and likely to survive for several decades. Its existence
may evoke surprise, but neither interest nor angry protest" (*Davar,*
May 29, 1953).

The above attitude of Israeli Jews to Zionism is part of a
far more serious condition that is developing in their relation to
the Jews of the Diaspora. They have had it drilled into their
minds by the Zionists leaders in Israel that Jews of the Diaspora
who fail to respond to the call to come and help rebuild the land
are like the Israelites in the Wilderness who preferred the flesh-
pots of Egypt to freedom and national independence. As a consequence, *the Jews of Israel are alienating themselves from the
Jews in the Diaspora. That cannot continue for long without
the Jews in the Diaspora becoming alienated from those in Israel.*

The possibility of such a calamitous rift arising, and its ominous consequences, were long ago foreseen by Franz Rosenzweig,
when he wrote in 1917: "The Zionists will be lost, once they
lose touch with the Diaspora. Their contact with the Diaspora
is the only thing that makes them hold fast to their goal. Only
by realizing its connection with Berlin, Lodz, or some day if you
like, New York, Valparaiso and Tobalsk will Palestine remain
Jewish and also make life in the Diaspora really possible" (Nahum
N. Glatzer, *Franz Rosenzweig,* p. 54).

From an overall political point of view, Israel cannot remain
neutral in international affairs. It has to align itself with one of
the two conflicting power blocs, and that one must be the Western bloc. Even there it is not likely to fare too well, because of
the tendency of the Western bloc to patronize the Arab governments, unless the Jews in the countries of the Western bloc are
vigilant to prevent that tendency from being indulged in at the
expense of Israel. If the Jews in the Diaspora countries are to
assume that responsibility, they must have a stake in the survival
of Israel. *They certainly cannot have a political stake, but they
can and must be made to feel that their destiny as Jews is bound
up with the future of the State of Israel.* The last thing in the
world, therefore, that should be done to them is to alienate them
by making them feel delinquent in their duty as Jews, because
they do not wish to migrate to Israel.

All in all, there can be no wiser words concerning the present status of Zionism that those written by Ben Gurion in his
pamphlet *Jewish Survival* (Government Year Book, 1953, p. 36).

"Since the establishment of the State," says he, "Zionism has had to face a grave, perhaps a supreme test, and it has not passed it. When the choice was offered of coming up to Israel or remaining in the Exile, the Zionist masses and their leaders alike chose to remain. It was made abundantly clear that Zionism, in the form which it has taken since the establishment of the State, does not mean *aliya* and does not require any personal identification with the builders of Zion. Such is Zionism in America, England, South Africa and most West European countries. This fact should be seen clearly, with all its implications. Historical facts are not to be disapproved, condemned, or raged at. They must be understood and evaluated. Conclusions must be drawn from them in order to change and put right what has to be and can be changed and put right."

III

How is this crisis in Zionism to be overcome? Veteran Zionists answer that we have been mistaken in believing that there is but one Zionism, the Zionism of the Basle Platform on which European and American Zionists are united. Actually there have been two Zionisms, a European and an American. The European Zionism has as its avowed aim the ingathering of *all* Jews from the various lands of their dispersion. American Zionism is merely a philanthropic movement to secure a haven of refuge for harassed and persecuted Jews.

But now that the State of Israel depends largely upon American Jews for its consolidation, they should adopt European Zionism, for their own good as well as for that of the State of Israel. Thus argue the old-line Zionists. American Jews should learn to use their communal machinery, their cultural, religious and educational institutions to develop a genuine Zionist movement, aiming at a national revival which would find expression in "a consciousness of the essential unity of all Israel and of a spiritual and intellectual *hakhshara* for Israel" (Note the ambiguous use of the term "Israel"!—Livneh, *State and Diaspora*, p. 37). Only that kind of Zionist direction and spiritual purpose, it is maintained, would give unity to all Jewish activities and bridge the gap between Israel and American Jewry. Only an all-embracing effort toward ultimate transfer of all Jews to Eretz Yisrael would secure for the State of Israel the moral and material support that is urgently needed at the present time to enable it to survive the many dangers that threaten it.

To expect American Jews to subscribe to this narrow interpretation of Zionism is quixotic and harmful. Even in the past, Jews tended to strike deep root wherever they were allowed to live, though they had to pay a high price in discriminatory treatment of all kinds. In the United States and other democratic countries, Jews enjoy more freedom and opportunity to achieve a higher standard of security and comfort than they ever knew in East Europe. How can they be expected to nourish dreams of transplantation to Eretz Yisrael? Granted that they encounter even in those countries enough anti-Semitism to prevent them from feeling perfectly secure, particularly in the light of what happened in a country like Germany. But that danger is negligible as compared with that implied in the fanatical resolve on the part of the Arab League to destroy Israel. The possibility that the Western powers may turn out to be a "broken reed" at the critical moment is not at all remote.

Moreover, no American Jew will subscribe to any cause that may cast serious doubt on the wholeheartedness of his Americanism. What that implies we have no less an authority, both from the American and Zionist standpoint, than the late Justice Brandeis to remind us. "An immigrant is not Americanized," he wrote, "unless his interests and affections have become deeply rooted here" ("True Americanism" in *Freedom*—ed. by Ruth Nanda Anshen, p. 350). It was Hayim Greenberg, a European Zionist and a naturalized American citizen, and not a third or fourth generation American Jew, who, at the 1951 World Zionist Congress in Jerusalem, declared: "It would be wrong to say that Jews have not struck roots there (in America) . . . Mass emigration is not on the current agenda of American Jewry" (*Jewish Frontier*, Dec. 1951).

The average American Jew cannot take seriously a philosophy of life that asks him to contemplate a future in which he would be expected to renounce his American citizenship. His interest in a State like Israel, with all of the risks that it faces, has not only to be free of any such fantastic demands; it has to be aroused and kept alive by a faith that transcends all states.

"Are there not at least some American Jews," it will be asked, "who can be expected to renounce their American citizenship, even under those conditions?" Those who ask that question forget that no great movement can afford to count upon exceptional or marginal people. The first requirement it has to meet is to be translatable into a system of education. Those who write off permanent Jewish life in the Diaspora consistently demand that American Jews educate their children to look forward to migration to Israel as their ultimate goal. That is more than even *some* American Jews can be expected to do.

We can no longer afford to postpone the long-needed reorientation of Zionism. Otherwise the Jewish People is bound to be like a man unable to swim who is thrown into deep water, so that nearly everything he does in his struggle is the opposite of what would be effective. It will not do to persist in stubbornly ignoring the realities of human nature. *If Zionism exists for the Jews and not the Jews for Zionism, it has to adjust itself to what may reasonably be expected of them.*

Even in ancient times, while the main body of Jews was still in Eretz Yisrael, changes in the alignments of the powers in the Middle East always affected profoundly the nature and form of what was then the Jewish State. The resettlement of Eretz Yisrael by the Jews after the first Babylonian exile was, even for that time, slower than the present resettlement. That was due mainly to a new political configuration beyond the control of the Jews. The political center of the Middle East was transferred from Babylonia to Susa and Ecbatana. The effect of that transfer was sufficient to render Palestine economically and politically no longer desirable enough for most of the Jews in Babylon to take advantage of the opportunity to return to it. Nevertheless, there did not develop the least sense of estrangement between the Jews who returned and those who remained, or any feeling among the Jews of Palestine that those of Babylon were less authentically Jewish.

In our day, the Jews of the Diaspora cannot help feeling perfectly at home in those countries where they are accorded full civil rights. Denouncing their reluctance to emigrate to Israel as disloyalty to the Jewish People will not help. On the other hand, urging them not to get out of touch with the vital center of Jewish life nor to lose the sense of Jewish destiny might help. That, however, would require placing their participation in the up-building of Eretz Yisrael in an altogether different category from that of a political movement to further Jewish nationalism. Zionism as a movement to bring about a spiritual or religious revival of all Jews throughout the world would be fully entitled to ask the Jewish communities of the free countries to provide their quota of able-bodied and high charactered men and women to come to Israel either to live there permanently, or, at least, to devote several years to its service. Those who remain at home could then be expected to become personally involved in the fate and fortunes of Eretz Yisrael. As part of a spiritual movement, the demand for *halutzim* would no more be resented than the demand of the churches for missionaries to go to the ends of the earth to spread the Christian gospel.

IV

Zionists should realize that the question whether Diaspora is part of Jewish destiny is not merely a theoretical one. Upon the answer to that question depends whether or not American Jews will maintain their interest in the growth and prosperity of the State of Israel.

The question of what should be the attitude of Diaspora Jewry toward migration to Israel is but part of the highly complex problem of the status of the Jews as a corporate entity. Since the Jews themselves no longer have a clear idea of the cohesive force which is to sustain their corporate existence, non-Jews cannot be expected to know what is to the best interests of world Jewry in dealing with matters concerning Israel. Recently a high official in the State Department of the United States aired views about the relation of American Jews to Israel that betrayed an abysmal ignorance of what is at stake. Strongly deprecating the deep interest which American Jews display in the State of Israel, Henry Byroade took occasion to criticize them for regarding Israel "as a headquarters—or nucleus, so to speak, of world-wide groupings of people of a particular religious faith, who must have special rights within and obligations to the State of Israel." Not even the reply of Prime Minister Sharett was sufficient to make good the lack of clarity with regard to the relationship of Diaspora Jewry to the Jews in Israel, or to the State of Israel.

"The Jews," said Sharett in his reply to Byroade, "are a people—one people throughout the world—the members of which are loyal citizens of their respective states. This loyalty is unreserved, and there exists a world Jewish brotherhood which is based upon a common fate—in the past, in the present and in the future; there also exists a world-wide Jewish partnership in the construction of the State of Israel, and in the spiritual attachment to it; these are fundamental facts of Jewish life, integrated in the pattern of present day international realities.

"There are countries in the world where that brotherhood and partnership are prohibited and stifled by the application of state power. The United States is not, and we firmly believe, will never be, one of these. Without an understanding of these facts, it is impossible to comprehend the essence of Israel's emergence, nor the nature of the process which sustains her and creates a natural basis for her future."

The legitimacy of the interest that American Jews take in the welfare of Israel is effectively set forth in the foregoing statement. But that statement does not touch upon the feasibility or legitimacy of an extra-territorial Judaism, which would make it unnecessary for Diaspora Jewry to live with a sense of guilt at not looking forward to migration to Israel. Sharett, himself, however, contends that "without a full recognition of the natural and historic rules embodied in these facts, there is no possibility of reaching mutual understanding with this unique State. There is no state like it in the present international world, because there is no parallel to Jewish history in the annals of mankind." (This and the previous quotation are taken from the *Israel Digest* of May 24, 1954.) Why, then, do the Zionist leaders evince so little concern about achieving "a full recognition" of all that is implied for Jewry as a whole in the establishment of the State of Israel?

It would seem, at first sight, that interest in the upbuilding of the State of Israel may be maintained from a purely American point of view, without being made into a Jewish issue. The State of Israel, as a bridgehead of democracy in the Middle East, comes well within the category of countries concerning which former President Truman said: "All our citizens must play a part in the making of Point Four Program a success. Our missionary groups, our philanthropic and charitable agencies must continue the efforts they have been making over the years for the improvement of conditions in foreign lands—Our young people can find careers in the pioneering work of bringing technical assistance to those countries. Our unions and business organizations should enlarge their foreign contacts and bring the benefits of their experience to less developed countries" (*N. Y. Times*, June 29, 1951).

It must be remembered, however, that the fear of anti-Semitism so obsesses many of our people that they are certain to avoid anything that might render them suspect of using their Americanism as a cover for their Jewish interests. Such Jews, and their number is legion, would be willing to contribute their share towards implementing the Four Point Program in any country whatever—except Israel. Hence the need of a philosophy of Zionism that would not have to rely on any specific or temporary political interest, but would derive from the ultimate principles of human rights.

Since we Jews are unique as a corporate entity, and we seek to secure the existence of a "unique State", we owe it to ourselves and to the rest of the world to define the nature of our unity, and to make clear its historic and present claims. When Sharett, in replying to a statement made by an official of the United States Government, says: "The Jews are a people—one people throughout the world," he is either uttering a meaningless cliché, or a principle of the utmost significance. If the latter, then the term "people" which he uses denotes not a mere accidental conglomerate of human beings. Then, *it is a concept of a uniting bond which so far has not received official recognition, nor achieved general understanding.*

Before the end of the eighteenth century, which marks the advent of the Jewish emancipation, all Jews knew themselves, and were known by the rest of the world, as a "nation," which, though exiled from its land and dispersed among the other nations, possessed a status similar to theirs. But the term "nation" no longer connotes in our day what it did before the rise of modern nations. A nation in former times meant a group that, besides being the bearer of a distinctive civilization, was united by an actual, or fictious, blood kinship. That, together with the fact that one had to be identified with the Church in order to qualify as a member of the nation, precluded the acceptance of Jews as members or nationals by any nation other than their own.

Modern nations are such not by virtue of blood kinship, whether actual or fictitious, but by virtue of formal contract or decision to act as a body. The qualification of Church membership is no longer required. That change has rendered possible the admission of the Jews into the body politic of a modern nation. By availing themselves of that right, Jews have placed themselves in the position of having to redefine their own group status. The only attempt at redefinition has been that which was implicit in the replies given to the twelve questions put by Napoleon I to the Jewish notables who met in Paris in 1806. "The replies of the assembly," writes David Philipson, "showed clearly that the Jews were not 'a nation within a nation' " (*The Reform Movement in Judaism*, p. 20). That attitude of the assembly was formally endorsed by the Reform Rabbinical Conference which took place in Brunswick, Germany in 1844. Though Zionism rendered the Reform renunciation of Jewish nationhood a dead letter, it has at no time taken an official position with regard to the status of world Jewry as a whole. Consequently, if the Jewish emancipation made a riddle of the corporate character of Jews, the establishment of the State of Israel has transformed that riddle into an enigma.

So long as the corporate character of world Jewry remains an enigma, it will be impossible to determine whether the

Jews outside the State of Israel are in exile or merely in a condition of dispersion. If the former, it is their Jewish duty to look forward to migration to Israel as their ultimate goal. If the latter, they may look forward to self-fulfillment as Jews outside Israel.

If Jews maintain their traditional conception of nationhood as a matter of actual or fictitious blood kinship, then Israel may be a Jewish State, but it cannot be a modern democratic óne. If it is to be modern and democratic, Jews who do not subscribe to the Orthodox version of Judaism should not be compelled to submit in matters of personal status to the authority of the Rabbinate, and civil marriage, civil divorce, civil burial and civil succession should be permitted. The present state of uneasy compromise between the religious and non-religious elements in Israel was inevitable. Without it, the State could not have come into existence, nor have lasted even a year. But it can be nothing more than a temporary expedient.

For the Zionist movement to renew itself, its leaders have to broaden their outlook and learn to see Zionism in its historical setting, as part of the struggle of Jewish people to survive and to remain true to its destiny. In other words, *Zionism is contemporary Judaism in action.* Judaism in action means that the Jewish people is actively engaged in an effort to adjust itself creatively to the contemporary world. That Zionism is in a condition of crisis means that contemporary Judaism is in a condition of crisis, or that the Jewish people is failing in its efforts to survive, and that it is continuing to disintegrate, despite the establishment of the State of Israel and the many seeming evidences of revival in the Diaspora. In seeking, therefore, a solution to the crisis in Zionism, we should keep in mind also the need of solving the crisis in contemporary Judaism.

All this leads to one inescapable conclusion: *Zionism should henceforth treat the establishment of the State of Israel only as the first indispensable step in the salvaging of the Jewish people and the regeneration of its spirit. Actually to attain these objectives, Zionism has to be viewed not merely as a cultural and political movement, but also as a religious movement for our day.*

V

Zionism has been defined as "that movement in Jewish life which seeks to foster a capacity among Jews for the living of a more abundant Jewish life." So far that conception of Zionism has not even reached the talking stage. If it is ever to reach the action stage, we have to begin thinking and talking about that conception as soon as possible. To live a more abundant Jewish life, whether in Israel or outside, Jews will have to foster a form of religion, which will be relevant both to the past career of the Jewish People and to the spiritual needs and world outlook of the modern man. It will have to be a religion free from both creedal and clerical authoritarianism, and able to meet the moral and spiritual needs of our day.

Such a religion will necessarily have to allow for diversity of belief and practice. There will have to be room in it for different metaphysical assumptions and systems of ritual observance. It will have to be a liberal religion, in the sense of being tolerant towards revelational or authoritative religion, provided, of course, that those who subscribe to the latter are, in their turn, tolerant towards liberal religion. It is evident that many will question the feasibility of giving the term "religion" such wide latitude. That is why the consensus of an expert body of thinkers and scholars is needed to accord the status of religion to whatever form of spiritual self-expression people choose to designate as their religion. If religion is to unite men and nations, instead of dividing them as it does at present, it has to be cultivated in an atmosphere of freedom and spontaneity. It must have not political ties with government, either in Israel or in the Diaspora. A movement like Zionism should not bring it about that Jews who have won the right to live should lose the right to live according to the dictates of their conscience.

"The complete penetration of life by religion will only occur," says Karl Mannheim, "if those who represent the religious tradition are once more able to go back to the genuine sources of religious experience and do not think that the habitual and institutional forms of religion will suffice for the reconstruction of man and society" (*Diagnosis of Our Time*, p. 116).

Jewish civilization, in retaining its religious character, would
be merely acting upon the inherent logic of all religion, namely,
hat every culture or civilization, insofar as it seeks to advance the
ᴄause of universal humanity, thereby helps to establish God's
Kingdom on earth. All competitive religious claims to being in
sole possession of the truth about God and to being entrusted with
the mission to spread it, in the face of resistance, are incompatible
with the type of religion which the Jewish People will have to
evolve.

This is a far cry from the eschatological messianism not only
of the Jewish tradition, but even from that which Zionists like
Rabbi Zvi Hirsch Kalischer and Rabbi Abraham Isaac Kuk en-
visioned. "Messianism," like the term "religious" in the modern
life context, must denote that intellectual, moral and spiritual
revolution in men's way of life which would further the cause of
universal freedom, justice and peace.

*If Zionism is to become a modern religious or messianic move-
ment, it has to be spelled out in a platform that would constitute
a renewal of the covenants which have thus far maintained the
indivisibility of the Jewish people and have given direction and
meaning to its unity.* "Israel as just another small state in the
Near East," Nahum Goldmann writes, "cannot hope to capture
the imagination of the world. Israel as a consequence of the
unusual history of our people, as a serious attempt to establish the
raison d'être of our unique destiny, and to invest our martyrdom
with meaning, can reclaim the sympathies and enlist the support
of the most enlightened sections of world public opinion" ("Herzl
and the Jewish State," *Jewish Frontier,* September 1954). For
Israel "to capture the imagination of the world," it has to radiate
creative spiritual vitality to Diaspora Jewry.

The present crisis in Zionism is both the effect and the cause
of the crisis in Judaism. Both crises have their roots in the weakening of the will-to-live as Jews. It surprises and shocks some of us
to overhear young Jews in Israel, or coming from Israel, saying:
"We don't want to be known as Jews; we are Israelis." We should
not treat this symptom lightly. If such a symptom breaks out in
Israel, the sense of Jewish continuity or identity must evidently

be weakening. If, outside Israel, the will to Jewish survival has only its own momentum to draw on, it is bound before long to suffer exhaustion, and the Jewish People which it has kept alive through the centuries is bound to become moribund.

Zionism cannot build the State of Israel without the moral and material support of a vigorous world Jewry, any more than it is possible to launch a ship without a bottom. Speaking on Air Force Day, July 28, 1954, Prime Minister Sharett had occasion to declare: "We call upon the Jewish people in all parts of the world to tighten their bonds with us—and to stand by us at all times of trial and test."

American Jews cannot be expected to take their Zionism seriously, nor Israelis to be interested in Diaspora Jewry except as population feeder for Israel, as long as Zionist leaders fail to rethink the philosophy of the movement and are satisfied with its *ad hoc* remedies for organic ills. Zionism can no longer afford to remain a matter of mood. It has to be spelled out in specific doctrines and policies that call for specific remedies against the ills of Jewish life in Israel as well as outside it.

The responsibility for dealing with the twofold crisis rests on the Jews of Israel and of the Diaspora.

VI

A.

1. Only ignorance or prejudice can blind one to the social idealism which marked the first three or four waves of immigration to Eretz Yisrael. Their trials, sufferings and sacrifices, as well as their magnificent achievements in the face of the most heartbreaking obstacles of nature and man, have left an indelible imprint on the Jewish population. The future development in Israel will, in all likelihood, bear as much the stamp of their contribution to life in Israel as American civilization bears the stamp of the Anglo-Saxon settlers on the Atlantic coast of North America. Shall they be blamed for the cultural trend in Israel, which points to a complete break with historic Judaism and with Diaspora Jewry

of the present? Shall they be held accountable for the drift there
toward a kind of Levantine culture which has as little in common with historic Judaism as contemporary Greek life has with
ancient Hellenism?

"It is an odd but undeniable fact," says a perceptive observer
of Hebrew education in Israel, "that the new generation which
has been reared in a Hebrew atmosphere, has studied the Bible
at least in part and has grown up in a country that is also a
museum of archaeology, has little connection with the past. This
is true as far as religion is concerned, but the animosity is not
the brand of cool atheism so often found in an age which has
exalted science to the place of God. Neither is it the brand common among the rebels who left the *Yeshivot* in order to drink of
the fountain of Enlightenment. Among *sabras* we are faced with
a rejection coupled with a lack of knowledge, a knowledge which
is flat and emotional at the same time. . . . 'For us religion is
symbolized by the Galut Jew who is dirty and ugly,' they are apt
to comment blandly. The break with the past goes further; it
discards Zionism itself as something tedious which smacks of moral
exhortation. . . . In the case of Zionism as in the case of religion,
education has failed to provide a valid substitute. The numerous
complaints about the fading of the pioneering spirit are nothing
if not the result of the spiritual and mental void which widens
as more and more *sabras* come into their own.

"Hand in hand with mental and spiritual apathy goes the
ambivalent attitude toward everything beyond the borders of Israel,
everything overseas. The Jew of the *Galut* is looked upon as
inferior to the new and vigorous Israeli, and Israel achievements
are underlined at every opportunity. . . . Young people stoutly
refuse opportunities of going abroad, and hesitate to come back
once they are there. The lack of balance implies inability to define
the position of Israel in relation to the outside world in general
and the *Galut* in particular. A relation as ill defined and blurred
is Israel's relation to Jewish history—which includes the history of
the *Galut* whether we live it or not—and to Zionism in all its
phases" (Gerda Luft, "The Break with the Past," *The Jerusalem
Post,* Friday, June 5, 1953).

Fifty years prior to the foregoing report of the status of Jewish education in Eretz Yisrael, the late Moshe Smilansky reported in the periodical *Hatzofeh* of Warsaw (no/217) the substance of an address of Yosef Vitkin at the convention of teachers in Zikhron Yaakov. (That report is reproduced in *Hapoel Hatzair* of November 17, 1953.) In that address, entitled "The Relation of the School to the Environment," Vitkin wrestled with the problem of how Jewish religion should be taught in the school. On the one hand, he laid it down as a principle that the conventional religious studies must have no place in the school, and on the other, he urged the need of "implanting in the hearts of the pupils the poetic sentiments of religion." He admitted, however, that he did not know how such "a poetic religion" was to be taught, and he appealed for careful study of the problem. His appeal, apparently, went unheeded, else a half century of Jewish education should have led to a more wholesome condition than that reflected in the above quoted report.

Recently, a great forward stride was taken in the education of the children in the State of Israel when a uniform curriculum was adopted as compulsory for all government subsidized schools, to the extent of 75 per cent of their studies. The remaining 25 per cent is optional and may be conducted in accordance with the program of the party to which the majority of the children's parents belong. That marks a definite step in the direction of unifying the diverse elements of the population and fostering in the children a sense of national unity. But as far as inculcating those moral and spiritual values which would develop in them a sense of continuity with the Jewish People of history, and of a common destiny with the Jews throughout the world, of that there is not the slightest prospect.

It is regrettable that even Ben Gurion failed to seize the opportunity presented by that new Government regulation to suggest more universal and human values as the purpose of the new curriculum. Instead, he indicated that the values which that curriculum would seek to inculcate would be: the primacy of manual labor, the love of country and nation, physical courage and *halutziut* (the pioneering spirit). One may even question the wisdom

of treating these values as objectives of education at all (*Cf*. U.
Durleker, "The Fundamental Values in Public Education," *B'te-rem*, October 16, 1953). But there can be no doubt that making
them the *main* objectives is not likely to produce that type of Jew
for whom the Jewish people has waited and hoped the last nine-teen centuries.

What is actually happening to the Jews of Israel? Some time
ago, Professor Ernst Simon published an article in *Commentary*
entitled, "Are We Israelis Still Jews?" There he tells of a sixteen-year old *sabra*, who asked him: "What must I read in order to
determine whether I am still a Jew?" "In the State of Israel,"
adds Ernst Simon, "the birth of a human being, as a son to his
people, does not by itself make him a Jew. The sharp break with
the heritage of the past, expressed pragmatically in a scorn of
the *galut* image of the Jew that verges on Zionist anti-Semitism,
has reduced the role of tradition."

"The flight from Judaism," writes Professor S. H. Bergmann,
"which is the process of assimilation, is as strong in Israel as in
the Exile, save that it is engaged in here without remorse, because
it hides behind the facade of Hebrew" ("Israel and the Diaspora,"
Forum, 1953).

2. The *halutz* and workers' groups, having proceeded from the
very start with the conscious purpose of making the Jewish na-tional renaissance the occasion for establishing in Eretz Yisrael
a social order based on freedom and justice, should have exercised
sufficient political wisdom and ingenuity to forestall the dangerous
fragmentation of less than a million Jewish votes into seventeen
rival parties struggling for power. The bitter partisan spirit which
is inculcated in youngsters at an early age through school and
youth activities blinds them to the primacy of the more funda-mental national purposes. The hope of rendering large-scale
cooperation compatible with individual freedom is likely to come
to naught, in view of the increasing pressure which the political
party brings to bear on its members, a pressure that is exercised
through its control of his livelihood, his cultural opportunities and
even his leisure.

Great credit has to be accorded to the secularist elements in Israel. Though it is they who, in the main, laid the foundations of the State, they have been operating on the principle of coalition in the Government, and have made numerous unreciprocated concessions to the Orthodox group. On the other hand, the demands of the Orthodox grow with every such concession. Latterly, after having obtained what is virtually exemption from army duty for the young women, they now demand complete exemption from the draft for the young men who attend the *Yeshivot* or Talmudical schools. They base their claim upon the teaching that "the Torah is Israel's sword." To that they have recently added another demand, namely, that Orthodox judges appointed by the State should not be required to take the oath of allegiance to the State.

"The liberty of faith and conscience which the religious party demands for itself," writes Ben Gurion, "it is not prepared to grant, or is not capable of granting to others as well" (*Jewish Survival*).

3. To be sure, in Israel the principal blame for the crisis in Judaism as the civilization of the Jewish People rests on those Jews who unqualifiedly spurn all traditional Jewish values. But the truth is that the intransigeance of the traditionalist Jews in Israel also bears a large share of the responsibility for the deplorable condition of Judaism there. They pursue policies and resort to public measures which are bound to alienate from Judaism all who find the supernaturalistic, authoritative world of the traditionalist mentally and spiritually suffocating.

We can afford to disregard a lunatic fringe like the *Neturé Karta*. But we must hold responsible the politically minded Mizrahi, the Agudah elements and the Rabbinate. Those elements insist upon being accorded privileges and exemptions from obligations to the State that are not granted to the rest of the population. And that is the least serious aspect of their offense against reason and justice. Far more serious are the parasitism and cynicism inherent in their religious intransigeance, as pointed out time and time again by Yeshaia Leibowitz, the founder of the religious workers group in the Jewish Labor Federation (*The Jersualem Post*, Friday, September 19, 1952).

He maintains that Rabbinic *Halakha* was formulated on "the supposition that the Jewish people in actual history lacks national independence and national functions and that, therefore, the Jew is not burdened by the duties and responsibilities of a citizen of a State." Leibowitz has the courage to debunk the claim that has always been made for traditional Judaism, that it is "a comprehensive and all embracing system and way of life." The situation in Israel has proved to the hilt that the Rabbinic tradition "fails to teach and to instruct how to run this State and how to perform, according to the Torah, the essential national and social functions under the given circumstances."

"Hence religious Jewry," continues Leibowitz, "has entangled itself in contradictions and equivocations, detrimental to the character and the honor of the Torah, even from the view of the religious—especially the religious youth—and utterly degrading the Torah in the view of non-religious or still undecided sections of the nation." He then proceeds to state in detail the many ways in which the religious Jews are enabled to adhere to their way of life "only at the price of a conscious approval of religious transgression by the State and the Nation as a whole." They can afford to observe the Shabbat only because the employees of the State run the waterworks and the electric works during that day.

There is not the slightest indication that Yeshaia Leibowitz's words are having any effect. It is doubtful if they ever will, because he operates with the traditional beliefs and values that assume the supernatural origin of the Torah and the immutability of the Rabbinic interpretation of its laws. He assumes that it is possible to expand the Torah within the framework of the tradition, to meet conditions never contemplated by it, and such as are presented by citizenship in a modern State. He further assumes that it is possible for religion, as a detailed regimen of individual living, to be part of the law of a modern State.

But Leibowitz has brought to the surface the disheartening fact that *the State of Israel, as at present constituted, holds out no prospect of making any contribution to the much needed re-*

orientation of Jewish life as a whole, whether in Israel or in the Diaspora. It is certainly futile to expect Marxist Mapam, or the various traditional groups, including the Mizrahists, Agudists and other uncompromising groups, to develop in Eretz Yisrael a Jewish community that might serve as a source of inspiration to the rest of Jewry to live a Jewish life.

The fact is that Israel is at present a multi-community State. Besides a Moslem community and a Christian community, there are two Jewish communities: on the one hand the coalition of the Mapai and the Orthodox Jews, and on the other a new Marxist community, known as Mapam. There is even the beginning of a Hebrew or Canaanite community which is ashamed to be associated with Jews, in Israel or outside. There are also the General Zionists, but outside of being opposed to socialism and in favor of private enterprise, they possess no specific philosophy or ideology concerning Jewish destiny or Jewish religion. *Mapai is the only group which has the potentiality of developing into a modern Jewish nation in Israel, but it lacks the will or even the understanding to create the nucleus of an international Jewish people.*

Accordingly, what else besides humanitarian or philanthropic good-will can motivate American Jews to strengthen the State of Israel? How long can that good-will last? Can we expect that philanthropic spirit, which is still prompted by a sense of kinship with fellow Jews, to carry over even to the present young generation of American Jews? How long can the Jews of Israel be willing to accept aid on those terms from the Jews of the Diaspora? These questions indicate the responsibility of the Jews of Israel in the two-fold crisis of Zionism and Judaism.

B.

Diaspora Jewries are in a state of moral and spiritual crisis, and their drift to assimilation is being daily accelerated. That fact is quite patent, except to those who deliberately shut their eyes to what is taking place about them.

About a century ago, the disintegration of Central European Jewry and its gradual absorption began to assume major proportions. "As long as the Jewish *massif* of Eastern Europe was in existence," writes Jacob Lestchinsky, "it, from time to time, introduced into Central Europe fresh groups of Jews with their traditions and heritage of Jewish stiffneckedness. These served as an auxiliary factor delaying the process of assimilation and preventing it from becoming complete."

It is against this background that we should evaluate the present condition of American Jewry. In the year 1880, we are told, only 275,000 Jews were to be found on the whole American continent, as compared with the present six million, or 52.9 per cent of the entire Jewish population in the world. Whatever Jewish life exists is largely due to the emigration of Jews from the Old World, "with their traditions and heritage of Jewish stiffneckedness."

As soon as replenishment from without ceases, Jewish life tends to disintegrate. "Reports from England are distinctly gloomy," we are told. "There are many mixed marriages; there is a biological deficiency in the higher and middle classes." The problem of mixed marriages in England "has become so grave that the Rabbinical Council was compelled to prohibit such weddings in synagogues under its supervision." The Whitechapel district, "which for decades furnished the Jewry of all England with modern Jewish culture and a living contact with Jewish world movements," is played out as a cultural Jewish influence. "Barely 40 per cent of all children of school age receive a Jewish education." "In Denmark, there are up to 60 per cent mixed marriages and 40 per cent in Switzerland."

Very few would disagree with the statement by C. Bezalel Sherman (quoted by Professor S. H. Bergmann, "Israel and the Diaspora," in *Forum*) that "the more Jewish citizens are concerned with the affairs of the lands in which they are born, the greater the part they play, in common with the remainder of the population, in fundamental values which do not derive from their Jewish heritage, the stronger grow the factors leading to the breaking up of the Jewish people."

The noted Jewish sociologist Aryeh Tartakower is no less apprehensive regarding the Jewish future. "We succeeded in preserving the unity of Israel for hundreds and thousands of years," he is quoted as saying, "yet nowadays the slogan of 'Every man to his tent! O Israel' is steadily fragmentizing the nation. Now we remain a people without a language, without a national culture, without a tradition. How shall we preserve our existence, if the soul of the nation has departed?"

All of the foregoing statements describe in objective and collective terms the present disintegration or moribund condition of the Jewish People. The degree of vitality possessed by the Jewish People is the resultant of the way the individual men and women who constitute it feel about being assimilated in the general population. Whether the Jewish People is alive, moribund, or dead, depends upon the extent to which individual Jews not only wish, but act upon the wish, to perpetuate Jewish life, Jewish association, and Jewish co-operation for common objectives. From that standpoint, Jews may be classified into groups like the following:

Those who are eager to be assimilated. As far as they are concerned, the Jewish people should follow the example of Charles II, who, lingering for a long time on his deathbed, apologized to his courtiers for taking too long a time to die.

Those who are torn by inner conflicts. They are like the Negro in the song, "Ole Man Riber"—who is "tired o' livin', and afeared o' dyin',"

Those who really want the Jewish people to live. They are the survivalists. According to a rough estimate, they amount to no more than fifty per cent of the Jewish population outside Israel. To them apply the words of the Psalmist, who declared, "I will not die but live, and recount the works of the Lord." This group itself, may be further subdivided, in accordance with the emphasis that is placed on different phrases in this verse.

For some survivalists, the will to live as Jews is confined to a reluctance to see the Jewish people die out. They emphasize the *lo amut,* "I will not die"; they do not assert their Judaism in positive terms. They trust the momentum of the past to continue Jewish life and are troubled only when someone in the family marries a non-Jew. Then they begin to realize that the path of least resistance may lead to complete dejudaization.

The rest of the survivalist group seek a program of action that will insure the survival of the Jewish people. Of these, some look upon survival itself as a sufficient goal, regardless of the kind of life that is perpetuated. They are the secularists, who stress the *ki ehyeh,* "but I will live," without, however, adding, *va'asaper ma'asei yah,* "and I will recount the works of God." Others, with a religious outlook on life, are only concerned with maintaining those religious rites and customs that bear witness to their faith in God and enable them to "recount" and proclaim His works. They are interested in maintaining synagogues, religious schools and rabbinical seminaries.

The old-line Zionists belong to the last two named groups of survivalists. The secularists wish to build a modern socialist democratic state; the religionists, a theocratic state. Both groups assume that there can be no future for Judaism outside Israel. *Were that true, or were that to become generally accepted, it is questionable whether the State of Israel would be able to survive the resulting loss of interest in it on the part of Diaspora Jewry.* And even if it will manage to survive, it is doubtful whether it will retain, for long, an authentically Jewish character.

The Jews are currently celebrating the tercentenary of their arrival on the American continent, but the future of their corporate existence and their religio-cultural heritage is far from assured there. The following are some of the facts that render it questionable. With no distinctive cultural values to mark Jewish life, we might expect Jews to fall back upon religious values as an outlet for their Jewishness. They build synagogues and establish religious schools for their children. But it does not require much insight to discern the almost desperate mood in which Jews seek this mode of escape from their spiritual isolation and moral *anomie.* Nor does one have to be a prophet to foresee the inevitable frustrations which must follow their discovery that though their spiritual leaders have long abandoned supernaturalism they have not replaced it with any other dedicated faith. The spiritual vacuum created by the growing desuetude of Orthodoxy cannot be filled by institutional loyalties and organizational slogans which are, so far, the most that the Reform and the Conservative Synagogues have to offer.

"We should not confuse," says a Reform rabbi, "increase in membership or institutional strength with a return to religion, nor the growth of parochial schools, nor the multiplication of synagogues and synagogue centers—all a manifestation of what has been termed the Jewish edifice complex" (Jacob J. Weinstein, *Proceedings, Central Conference of American Rabbis,* 1953, page 298). Despite the noise about the increase of religious schools, only a limited number of parents give their children some kind of Jewish schooling and only in rare instances does that schooling give a positive Jewish bent to their way of life. The Jewish religious schools are like subway trains always full, with people constantly getting on and getting off at every station. The number of men and women who are *qualified* to teach Jewish subject matter is shockingly small (*Cf. Religious Education,* Sept.-Oct. 1953 issue on "Protestant, Catholic and Jewish Education").

The following summary of American Jewish life by a Reform rabbi who was president of the Central Conference of American Rabbis speaks for itself: "The state of Jewish culture is low among American Jews. . . The average Jewish businessman and professional man is illiterate Jewishly. . . The great majority of Jews, like the great majority of non-Jews prefer entertainment to serious study and thought. Synagogues and centers are busy, but much of their acivity is designed for the box office.

"And what about our gifted Jews? How many of them are affiliated with a synagogue? How many attend? Can names like Brandeis, Einstein, Hillman, Lilienthal, Oppenheimer, etc., be associated with any type of normative Judaism?

"Is this not also true of our ablest youth? How many of our bright young Jews are really interested in Judaism or Jewish culture? How much *Kavanah* is to be found in the American Jewish heart? Do the great synagogue buildings express greatness of soul or fatness of purse?

"How many Jews live in their Judaism? Ask any Orthodox or Conservative rabbi how many of their people observe, really observe, Kashrus and the Sabbath, which they profess to believe in. Ask any Reform rabbi the extent to which his congregants'

lives are directed by Judaism" (Philip Bernstein, "New Year
Message" *Opinion*, September-October 1954).

Another factor which accounts for the disintegration of the
Jewish People is the failure to grapple with the problem of retaining Jewish group individuality. Jews cannot afford to be segregated from the cultural life of their country, without detriment
to themselves and their country. On the other hand, if integration
is not to spell complete absorption and disappearance, Jews have
to find a way of retaining some measure of group autonomy. That
implies possession of some sort of group status *vis-a-vis* the rest of
the world. Most Jewish leaders have ignored that need. The few
who have recognized it, have minimized its importance.

Jews at present resemble a demobilized army. Now more than
ever we experience the ominous significance of what the Hebrew
poet Judah Leib Gordon said about the Jewish People: "We are
neither a people nor a religious community; we are only a human
herd." With the decay of supernaturalistic religion as a uniting
bond, no other inner cohesive force has thus far been generated.
Jewish unity, whatever of it still exists, is buttressed from *without*
by the Christian tradition and by its offspring anti-Semitism, but
its *inner* supports are crumbling.

"It is rather difficult to describe positively the character of
the Jewish group as a whole," writes Kurt Lewin. "A religious
group with many atheists? A Jewish race with a great diversity
of racial qualities among its members? A nation without a state
or a territory of its own containing the majority of its people? A
group combined by one culture and tradition, but actually having
in most respects the different values and ideals of the nations in
which it lives? There are, I think, few chores more bewildering
than that of determining positively the character of the Jewish
group. It is not easy to see why such a group should be preserved
as a separate unit, why it has not entirely given up its will to
live, and why the nations have refused to grant Jews full assimilation" (*Resolving Social Conflicts*, p. 180). *As long as that situation obtains, Jews are without spiritual anchorage.*

It is futile to expect Zionism, as a movement to consolidate
the State of Israel, and Judaism, as the religious civilization of

the Jewish People, in their present condition, to reinforce each other. Before they can have that mutual effect, they will have to undergo considerable rethinking and replanning.

VII

Zionism has to be redefined, so as to assure a permanent place for Diaspora Judaism. Such a redefinition, while affirming the indispensability of Eretz Yisrael as the home of Judaism for Jews throughout the world, would have to stress the peoplehood, or the oneness and indivisibility, of world Jewry. On the other hand, the Jewry of Israel as nuclear to and interactive with the Jewries of the Diaspora would have to be recognized as a permanent condition.

We need a new kind of Zionism, a Zionism which will enable the entire Jewish people to cope with the problem of survival and growth under circumstances that threaten its existence as it has never been threatened before. To be sure, the revival of Eretz Yisrael as the homeland of Judaism is a *sine qua non* of the continued existence of the Jewish people, but it is not sufficient. There exists just as great a possibility of dejudaization in Eretz Yisrael as outside it, because there are at present no intellectual or spiritual barriers to halt the dejudaizing process.

For Zionism to halt this process—and no less a purpose can keep Zionism alive—it must reckon not only with the fact that the Jewish People, like every living body, has to interact with the surrounding world, but also with the fact that the interaction has henceforth to be of a different kind from what it was in the past.

Why is that? Because in the past the surrounding world only touched Jewish life peripherally. Now that world has so invaded Jewish life that it penetrates it interstitially, as it were. *The world is more with us than we Jews are at present prepared for.* The ambivalence of the world, its being both food and poison, requires of us Jews far more discernment, self-control and self-sacrifice than it ever did before. What Jewish cause, if not Zionism, is likely to bring out these traits in us?

As long as Jews had to deal with a surrounding world that affected them only peripherally, the religious tradition supplied

them both the rationale and the guidance for their segregation
from the rest of the world. With the surrounding world, however,
invading Jewish life interstitially, segregation is out of the question. In place of segregation, Jews look to integration. But if
the integration is not to mean being swamped by the surrounding
world, then it must give rise to a style of living which may be
termed living in "two civilizations." For that, the tradition has
not prepared us. Only a movement which dares to face the new
realities in the world about us is likely to help us achieve that
new style of living. That is the task of the New Zionism.

The New Zionism should make it possible for us to see Jewish life steadily and whole. It should relate the Jewish people,
the Jewish religion and the Jewish way of life to Eretz Yisrael as
the *alpha* and *omega* of Jewish existence. Eretz Yisrael has to be
reclaimed as the only place in the world where Jewish civilization
can be perfectly at home. But also other lands where Jews have
taken root have to be rendered capable of harboring that civilization. The one purpose cannot be achieved without the other.
*Should Jewish civilization fail to be at home in Eretz Yisrael, it
will disappear everywhere else. Should it disappear everywhere
else, it is bound to give way to some new Levantine civilization
in Eretz Yisrael.*

VIII

Both Zionists and their forerunners, the *Maskilim,* or the
Jewish cultural nationalists, were, no doubt, aware of the shattering
impact of the modern world into which Jews moved as soon as
they began to be emancipated. But, with the exception of Ahad
Ha'am, their diagnosis usually amounted only to identifying the
symptoms rather than the basic causes of the crisis. Such a diagnosis, for example, was that of Jacob Klatzkin. In discussing the
difference between the old *Galut* and the new, he added: "In the
old *Galut,* Judaism had its sure support in that portable state
founded upon a religious constitutionalism which had not only
been saved, but was capable of creative expansion. Hence territorial settlement and delimitation was not a necessary condition
of its life. Its love and loyalty clung to the land of the fathers;

it consumed itself in yearning for the sod. But these were not the exercise of a pregnant and creative will. Yet this was possible because (the People) Israel lived in perfect faith of its own indestructibility in exile. So long as this faith and this sense of security had power, the will had no incentive to creative tension. It is otherwise in the *Galut* of modernity. The old faith and security are gone" (*Jewish Frontier*, September 1942).

It is no wonder, therefore, that the conclusion which he drew from his diagnosis was that the only remedy was escape from *Galut*. He wished Jews were in a position to punish as traitors anyone who obstructed the Zionist movement, as false prophets those who maintained that there was a future for Judaism also in the Diaspora. He could not possibly imagine that crisis might overtake Judaism even in Eretz Yisrael.

The truth is that the breakdown of the religious constitutionalism upon which the Jews had founded their "portable state," when the Second Commonwealth was destroyed in 70 C.E., is merely a symptom of a universal breakdown of the supernaturalistic universe of values upon which that "religious constitutionalism" itself had been based. What guarantee did Klatzkin or any of the secular Zionists have that the modern *Galut* would not so completely abandon the traditional miracle-founded hope of a return of the Jewish People to Eretz Yisrael as to leave no room even for any desire to return as a modern nation? From a purely secular standpoint, whatever permanent spiritual values the Jewish People evolved in the past have become part of the universal mind and did not require that the Jewish People should come to life again.

From the moment that Jews began to look to "Enlightenment" to qualify them for citizenship and integration into the nations of Europe and America, they were being propelled into a mode of life and thought in which their traditional values, whether national or religious, social or personal, no longer applied. Ever since then Jews have found themselves in a mental climate which negates the supernaturalistic and other worldly assumptions concerning salvation. The new climate of opinion affirms that some kind of humanist religion like nationalism, or socialism, or

the combination of both, is the only source of man's salvation.
It is now generally assumed that, whatever else salvation may
mean, it has to include physical, mental, moral and spiritual
maturity. The means to attain these desiderata are foresight, ambition and self-reliance—qualities of character which were suspect,
or at least deprecated, in the pre-modern traditional other-worldly
outlook on life.

So far, we have no philosophy either of Zionism or of Judaism to give body to the fact so boldly and sharply stated by Ben
Gurion: "With the birth of the State, a fundamental change has
come about in the way we see ourselves and the world and the
way the world sees us. Our inner and outer nature is being
fashioned anew." Indeed very little has been done to fashion our
inner and outer nature intelligently and creatively. That little is
entirely out of proportion to the cataclysmic changes that have
taken place in the world about us.

As Jews we have to stake our existence as a People upon
the ultimate establishment of societies, whether nations, churches
or peoples, on the basis of universal freedom, justice and peace.
The transition from supernaturalistic and authoritarian society to
a naturalistic and democratic society is bound to be slow and
checquered. We cannot afford, however, to let every reactionary
wave make us doubt the actual direction of the tide.

An objective study of the large numbers of intellectuals and
middle class people who were allured by communism, reveals that
they were drawn to it, because they had thought they saw in it a
practical way of implementing their idealism, their sense of justice
and hope for universal peace. The fact that communism has had
to make use of the slogans of equality and democracy to win its
way into the hearts of the masses proves the soundness of the
common man's soul.

To be sure, commitment to the cause of a free, just and peaceful society in a troubled world is bound to involve us Jews in
many a sacrifice and frustration. But if we wish to live a meaningful life, we have to put our trust in the high potentialities of
human nature and in their ultimate fulfillment, and to realize
that such trust is synonymous with trust in God. Whatever else

the belief in God may mean to us Jews, its main significance has to be that of belief in a Power that makes for man's becoming fully human. Unless that belief becomes the main drive in everything that we do as Jews, the sooner we become absorbed by the general population the better.

As Zionists, we have to reconstitute our peoplehood, reclaim our ancient homeland and revitalize our Jewish way of life. Each of these three objectives should be pursued with the end in view, both in Israel and in the Diaspora, of developing such interpersonal and intergroup relations as are likely to help us become more fully human. That is to be our religion and our mission.

"The Jewish people, as such," Nahum Goldmann stated recently, "has no position with regard to the socio-economic ideologies of our time. . . However, being outside this conflict as a people, we demand the right to live as Jews and to educate our children as Jews in every part of the world and within every social system in the world." He refuses, however, to absolve us from the problems that are forced on us as Jews as well as on our neighbors by increasing industrialization, increasing centralization of economic and military power, increasing world interdependence and the rise of totalitarianism. No wonder he finds it necessary to add the following: "Let us be on our guard in a common front with all who adhere to the ideas of human freedom, of individual liberty and intellectual tolerance. It is our destiny—it should be our willing obligation—to be everywhere in the forefront of the fight for these ideas, even when those ideas are unfashionable or unpopular. These alone can create a climate in which we live, and so long as they are threatened anywhere in the world, our position will remain unsafe" (*Status of Jewry*, World Jewish Congress, 1953).

What Goldmann states in social terms were stated more specifically by Franz Rosenzweig in reference to Eretz Yisrael: "The spirit of this spiritual center cannot grow in the direction of pure uninhibited nationalism avid for its own development, no matter how much it would like to. Just because of its focal character it must constantly keep in sight the periphery which can never be governed by pure nationalism, but will always be constrained to

regard the national as a function of the religious, and for very
simple reasons based on the sociology of minorities" (Glatzer,
Franz Rosenzweig, page 269).

Nothing less than a large-scale effort on the part of Jews
in Israel to adopt the ideals of a Moses Hess, an Ahad Ha'am,
an A. D. Gordon, a Berl Katznelson, and a Martin Buber to the
realities of our modern mass civilization, and to incorporate those
ideals into the Israeli way of life will arouse Diaspora Jewry from
its lethargy, and impel it to invest its material and human resources in Israel.

Only the interaction of such Judaism and such Zionism will
evoke a sense of mutual responsibility from the Jews of Israel and
of the Diaspora.

BIBLIOGRAPHY

DAVID BEN-GURION, "Jewish Survival," Reprint from *The Government Year
Book, 5714 (1953-54)*.

——. *Rebirth and Destiny of Israel*, N. Y., Philosophical Library, 1954.

NORMAN BENTWICH, *Israel*, N. Y., McGraw Hill, 1953.

Facts and Figures, N. Y., Israel Information Service, 1953.

GERALD DE GAURY, *The New State of Israel*, N. Y., Praeger, 1953.

NAHUM GOLDMANN, *Status of Jewry*, World Jewish Congress, 1953.

Israel, Government Year Book, 1953-54, Jerusalem, Government Printer.

OSCAR KRAINES, *Israel:* "The Emergence of a Policy," Parts I-II, *The Western
Political Quarterly*, September-December 1953.

HAL LEHRMAN, *Israel: The Beginning and Tomorrow*, N. Y., Sloane, 1951.

EMIL LENGYEL, *World Without End: The Middle East*, N. Y., Day, 1953;
includes a section on Israel.

ELIEZER LIVNEH, *State and Diaspora*, Jerusalem, Modern Israel Library, 1953.

RAPHAEL PATAI, *Israel Between East and West*, Phila., Jewish Publication Society,
1953.

ERNST SIMON, "Are We Israelis Still Jews," *Commentary*, April 1953.

The Background of Pre-State Zionism

I

TO AVOID ANY MISUNDERSTANDING of the Zionist movement, what Nahum Goldmann has recently written about it should be borne in mind. "Zionism," he says, "was always far more than a nationalistic political movement" ("Herzl and the Jewish State," *Jewish Frontier,* September 1954). Zionism has sought to be nothing less than a means to the regeneration of the Jewish people. At the present time, therefore, the aim of Zionism should be to make Israel secure as the home of the Jewish religious civilization and to strengthen Diaspora Jewry against the disintegrating influences of its environment. To achieve that goal, Zionism has to reckon, on all levels of human life, with the principal factor that threatens the disintegration of the Jewish People. That factor is preeminently a cultural one, with psychological effects that undermine Jewish life.

It is impossible to determine just what is needed to keep the Jewish People alive, unless we realize the full extent of the cultural as well as spiritual cataclysm which struck it when it began to be emancipated from the status of alienage and to be incorporated into the body politic of the Western nations.

Not only has the entire topography of Jewish life been changed, but the very climate of opinion in which, so to speak, Jews have to breathe is no longer what it always had been. The Western world, where most Jews had lived, was, in pre-modern times, affirmatively Christian in its outlook. Its climate of opinion, though hostile to the Jewish People, consisted mainly of beliefs, habits and values originating in Jewish tradition. In the Christian

universe of thought, the Jewish People occupied the central position, even though it was one of obloquy.

To this very day, Christian theologians who think and speak
in the traditional language stress that fact. John Baillie, for example, the English theologian, writes: " 'In those days it shall
come to pass that ten men from nations of every language shall
take hold of the skirt of one Jew, saying 'We will go with you
for we have heard that God is with you.' These words are those
of Zechariah, the prophet, and they have come true in a wider
sense than he was able to foresee. For countless men and women
of every tongue and nation, the story of the Jews is now sacred
history, and the land of the Jews is their Holy Land" (*Invitation
to Pilgrimage,* p. 66). A noted biblical scholar writes in a similar
vein. "Not only do we draw," he says, "our earliest and deepest
social and moral—not to mention religious—concepts from the
experiences of ancient Israel. But throughout its entire history, western European civilization has maintained the Bible as the central
document of its cultural inheritance" (Edward Whiting Fox,
"Foreword" to *Ancient Israel,* by Harry Orlinsky).

The foregoing statements are hardly representative of the
contemporary climate of opinion. The recent testimony of the
Rev. Dr. Joseph L. Hromadka before the 400 delegates of the
World Presbyterian Alliance is a far more reliable index of the
present state of Christendom. "The historical structure of this
(Christian) civilization finds itself in agony. It is a situation of
far reaching significance for the ecumenical movement. Unless we
understand its meaning, we can hardly face adequately our present challenge. In this respect, our situation greatly differs from
that of the Reformation era; yes, indeed it greatly differs from
the world atmosphere of the days of some thirty to forty years
ago. . . . Many of us can hardly free ourselves from the delusion
of the Christian countries' being even today masters, arbiters and
leaders of the world. However, we have to see clearly the very
movement of history, and avoid any self-deception. We have to
sense the imperceptible yet real shifting of the center of gravity
from the Christian nations to the non-Christian world. . . . The
so-called Christian civilization finds itself in disintegration." On

that same day, another prominent churchman, the Most Rev.
Geoffrey Francis Fisher, was reported as complaining, before the
Anglican Congress assembled at Minneapolis, Minnesota, of "the
mounting forces of power groups of mass direction and of man's
obsession with materialism which blind them to the next world"
(*New York Times*, Thursday, August 5, 1954).

The realm of discourse referred to by the theologians as still
dominant, and by the churchmen as disintegrating, actually began
to go into eclipse as far back as the end of the seventeenth century,
since which time, according to Arnold Toynbee, "Western Christendom has been progressively discarding its ancestral religion"
(Magazine Section, *N. Y. Times*, Sunday, December 26, 1954,
page 25). It is as different culturally and spiritually from the realm
of discourse into which Western mankind has been moving as the
astronomical universe of Ptolemy is different from the astronomical
universe of Copernicus. Whereas in the past, the authoritative
tradition, based on the teachings of the Bible, had the first and
last word in all human questions, today it has nothing to say in
answer to the questions by which we seek to orient ourselves to
reality.

Add to this the fact that no population or human society can
any longer live in complete isolation from any other, that contact,
commerce, and culture interlock the lives and fates of men and
nations. Human activities were once influenced to a large extent,
consciously or unconsciously, by the assumption that salvation was
to be achieved in "the next world." Today the world in which
men are learning to seek their salvation is the here and now, the
world which is lived, suffered and enjoyed. Even those who, on
Sabbaths and festivals, in churches and synagogues, pray and
discourse in terms of a supernatural and God-centered universe of
ideas and values—and even *their* number is on the wane—plan
and act the rest of the time in their homes, schools, shops and
offices in terms of a natural and man-centered universe of ideas
and values. "For 300 years," says Henry Steele Commager, "Cal-
vinism had taught the depravity of man without any perceptible
effect on the cheerfulness, kindliness and optimism of Americans.
Whatever they have said or sung, they preferred this life to the

next, and when they imagined heaven, they thought of it as
operating under the American Constitution" (*The American Mind,*
p. 162).

That change in attitude accounts for a radically different
conception of man's future on earth. Even as late as the eighteenth
century. whenever thinkers speculated on that future, they were
certain it could be merely a continuation of the present, with all
its evils and frustrations. It never occurred to them that the conditions of human life might be so altered as to give rise to many
a good that seemed absolutely impossible. The notion of progress
was unknown in pre-modern universe of thought.

The Enlightenment brought about a new dynamic concept
of reality and a transvaluation of values. With the confidence that
man acquired in his ability to extend the boundaries of knowledge
and experience came faith in reason and in progress. Despair was
replaced by hope. It is true that much has happened since then
to dampen man's high spirits and to cast him once again into
gloom. Anti-rationalism and supernaturalism seem to be coming
to the fore again. Now the thinking men and women seem to be
straddling two incongruous realms of being, victims of intellectual
and spiritual schizophrenia. That condition, however, cannot last.
Sooner or later people will come to their senses. Reason and hope
will reassert themselves. *Faith in progress as automatic will be
replaced by the realization that progress has to be rationally and
spiritually willed. Once again, men will strive to make life in this
world significant and worthwhile. That is the kind of future in
which we have to find a place for the Jewish People.*

II

The consequences to the Jewish People of its emancipation
from civic disabilities, and of its efforts to integrate its life and
thought with the life and thought of the Western nations, have
been shattering. The realm of ideas and values which Jews and
non-Jews inhabited before the middle of the eighteenth century
was, by and large, a product of the Jewish spirit. On the other
hand, the realm of ideas and values which Jews and non-Jews

have since come to inhabit is a product of the same Greek spirit which a long time ago threatened to destroy Judaism. Having found fulfillment after the Middle Ages in the Humanist Renaissance and in various social, industrial, and political revolutions since then, the ancient Greek spirit has come to be far more formidable, and its threat to contemporary Judaism far more ominous.

The immediate psychological impact of so radical a change upon the attitude of Jews toward their own People and its tradition could only be one of bewildering disorientation. Gone was the sense of inner peace and security in the awareness that the Jewish People had provided the rest of mankind with a world outlook and a sense of values that were an indispensable means to salvation. Even though the rest of mankind were hostile, they had to justify their hostility in terms of that very world outlook and sense of values. The feeling of disillusionment and the loss of self-respect that invaded the soul of the Jew when his spiritual universe seemed to cave in like a house of cards might have been prevented, if Jewish spiritual leaders had possessed the wisdom to prepare their people for the shock of the change.

Fortunately, the Jewish People's will to live was strong enough to impel some of its articulate thinkers to seek to redress the lack of preparation, and to help it negotiate the dangerous transition from the pre-modern to the modern universe of thought and values. Those were the *Maskilim* (illuminati) or "enlighteners." They strove valiantly to orient their fellow-Jews to the modern realm of discourse, without loss of self-esteem as Jews. They constituted for the Jewish People in modern times what Arnold Toynbee designates as the "creative minority," which comes to the rescue of a society when it experiences crisis.

By no means all who joined the *Haskala* or Enlightenment movement gave that direction to it. Some gave it the very opposite direction. They added to the Jewish sense of inferiority and contributed to the defection from Judaism. Those, however, who sought to fortify the sense of Jewish self-respect may have come somewhat late along in the Jewish emancipation. Yet if it were not for their endeavors, there probably would have been no Zionist movement.

The fact which in all this discussion has an important bearing on the present crisis in Zionism is that *without the reorientation to Judaism and the Jewish people which the Haskala movement made possible, the Jews would have been totally unprepared for the Zionist movement.* It is true, as we shall see, that, due to the abortive character of the *Haskala* movement, the perspective of pre-State Zionism was necessarily limited. That limitation accounts in large measure for the crisis through which it is at present passing. The problem, therefore, boils down to the need to correct that perspective.

III

In order to comprehend fully just how far the *Haskala* movement saved the Jewish People from disintegration and paved the way for Zionism—though in neither purpose did it go far enough—we should familiarize ourselves with the revolutionary change which every aspect of human life in Western mankind has undergone as a result of the shift of salvational interest from the next world to this world, or from what may be termed the wish-world to the real world.

In the first place, we must realize that the pre-modern Judaism by which our forebears lived was uncompromisingly other-worldly. The frequent denials of this fact on the part of Jewish scholars is motivated by an apologetic spirit; it develops in them a blind spot for all the texts in the tradition which shout the doctrine of other-worldliness. The plain truth is that traditional Judaism taught with all possible emphasis and clarity that man's salvation could not be achieved in this world. Whether one is to deny oneself the comforts and pleasure of this world and practice self-denial or asceticism is not relevant. What is more than relevant is the principle enunciated in *Avot,* and reiterated in different words all through Rabbinic literature, that this world is a portico which leads to the world to come.

The assumption that salvation is achievable only in the hereafter is stressed with equal emphasis in the philosophic writings of the authoritative Jewish theologians. Two instances will suffice to verify that. Saadia Gaon devotes one of the ten sections of his

Book of Beliefs and Opinions to the belief in the world to come. In addition to quoting Scripture and the oral tradition in support of that belief, he maintains that reason compels us to subscribe to it. "It is incompatible with God's character," he writes "that the measure of happiness reserved for the human soul be limited to this-worldly pleasure and well-being. For all well-being in this world is bound up with misfortune, all happiness with hardship, all pleasure with pain, and all joy with sorrow." Maimonides, in referring to the practice of the *mitzvot,* states that they are intended to inculcate peace of mind. Moreover, he adds, "they constitute the great good which God has caused to radiate for the cultivation of this world as a means of enabling man to inherit the world to come" (*Hilkhot Yesodei Hatorah,* 84).

The other-worldly realm of ideas and values, which was inhabited in common by Jews and non-Jews throughout the pre-modern era, consisted of much more than the complex of beliefs and practices which had to do with salvation. It included the entire Judeo-Christian tradition based on the Bible. It affirmed the historicity of the miraculous events recorded there. It assumed that God, as the creator of the world and of man, had revealed to man what he should do and what refrain from in order to be worthy of salvation. The natural order of things was deemed subject to change at any time God chose, and God might so choose for the sake of his loyal ones, or in answer to prayer. Man was not expected to discover the secrets of nature, and least of all to manipulate it. That was regarded as interfering with God's established order, and, therefore, as presumptuous. Religion was not only God-centered, with God conceived as transcendent and completely other, but supernatural in its origin and working. Its rituals and other practices assumed, to a large extent, the character of magic which ignored the inescapable necessities and inevitable conditions of life.

The foregoing description of pre-modern religion is introduced here not only for the sake of emphasizing the nature of the other-worldly realm of discourse which both Jews and non-Jews have been gradually abandoning. It should also serve as a reminder of the fact that *much of the difficulty in getting people to understand*

that religion is compatible with a naturalistic and humanist ap-
proach to human life and salvation is due to the unwarranted
assumption that the only kind of religion that is authentic is the
one that answers to the above description.

A Copernican revolution takes a much longer time getting
underway in universes of thought than it does in astronomy. The
former revolution dates from the latter half of the 15th century
when, with the Renaissance, man may be said to have rediscovered
himself, the first discovery having taken place in Hellenic civilization. New worlds, new peoples, new human possibilities began to
be discovered. Since then one revolution has followed close upon
the heels of the preceding, beginning with the commercial, which
was followed by the political, then the industrial, then the tech-
nological. Francis Bacon's formula, "Knowledge is power," has
been acted on to such an extent that man has come into possession of power which he can no longer control.

By the end of the eighteenth century, the medieval order of
society, with its clericalism and feudalism, began to give way to
the modern secularist order. Clericalism gave way to Enlightenment and feudalism to nationalism. Although both Enlightenment
and nationalism had their roots in the same spirit of revolt against
authoritarianism, the one spiritual, the other political, they did not
from the very start advance with equal pace. Due to the tendency
of the spiritual to lag behind the political growth, clericalism,
though very much weakened, is still very much of a force to be
reckoned with. In some instances it has even nourished rising
national cultures. On the other hand, nationalism today possesses
the prestige and power which other-worldly religion possessed during the early Middle Ages, the "age of faith."

In the meantime, out of the same revolt against authoritarianism that gave rise to Enlightenment and nationalism sprang
socialism. The industrial revolution, reenforced by the technologi-
cal, led to the questioning of the absolute or divine right of
property, especially when that property was an instrument of production. The questioning, which at first was carried on a moral
level, was transferred by Karl Marx to the level of power and
the struggle for its possession. At first it appeared that socialism

would displace nationalism as a substitute for traditional religion. Instead, events have so far shown that nationalism and traditional religion tend to reenforce each other, and each uses the other's emotional appeal to strengthen its own cause.

IV

The foregoing facts have a vital bearing on the vicissitudes of the Jewish People during the last century-and-a-half, and on their culmination in the Zionist movement. Enlightenment, nationalism and socialism have had an ambivalent effect on the Jewish People. On the one hand, they have been the chief factors of its disintegration. On the other hand, insofar as they have been put to the service of the Jewish People's will to live, they have not only fortified it, but have also created new instruments for its realization. One of the early leaders of the Enlightenment movement among Jews, Shalom Hakohen, the founder of *Bikuré Ha-Ittim,* a magazine which followed *Ha-Meassef,* himself espoused in his *Mattaé Kedem al Admat Tzafon* the cause of Jewish nationhood. Himself a *Maskil,* he denounced those who were led by Enlightenment to break with their Judaism.

What Enlightenment, nationalism and socialism have done to undermine Jewish life and alienate some of the most creatively gifted Jews from their people is everywhere evident. Dubnow in his history of "The Jews in Russia and Poland" describes the impact of modernism on the callow Jewish youth during the reign of Alexander II in the following words: "Many children of the ghetto rapidly enlisted under the banner of the Russian youth, and became intoxicated with the luxuriant growth of Russian literature which carried to them the intellectual gifts of contemporary European writers. The masters of thought in that generation, Chernyshevski, Dobrolubov, Pisaryev, Buckle, Darwin, Spencer became also the idols of the Jewish youth. The heads which had but recently been bending over the Talmud folios in the stuffy atmosphere of the *hadorim* and *yeshivot* (elementary and advanced religious schools) were now crammed with the ideas of positivism, evolution and socialism. Sharp and sudden was the transition from rabbinic scholasticism and soporific hasidic mysticism to this world of ideas, flooded with the light of science, to these new revelations announcing the glad tidings of the freedom of thought, of the demolition of all traditional fetters, of the annihilation of all religious and national barriers, of the brotherhood of all mankind" (Volume II page 209).

An account of the defection from the Jewish People, which was prompted by the centrifugal forces loosed by this-worldly striving for salvation, would constitute a history of the Jews far more tragic in character than the catalogue of tears and sighs recounting their martyrdom. To determine why these modern world movements have had that effect upon the Jewish People, and where the blame lies, might prove of great value in finding the needed remedy. *Yet the fact that those modern movements need not intrinsically have had that disintegrative effect on Jewish life has been amply demonstrated by the movement for Jewish cultural nationalism which arose in Eastern Europe.* The modern movements, however, could not *but* have had an ambivalent effect on the Jews. That becomes apparent when we consider their professed common purpose to help human beings realize to the utmost their latent capacities through the maximum use of their opportunities in this world.

"Enlightenment" was the term used in the 18th and 19th centuries to designate the transition from other-worldiness to this-worldliness, from supernaturalism to humanism. That transition expressed for those who lived through it a passing from immaturity to maturity, from authoritarianism to autonomy. "Enlightenment is a man's emergence from his immaturity," said Kant, "an immaturity for which he himself was responsible. Immaturity is the inability to use one's intelligence without another's guidance. One bears the responsibility for this immaturity, if its cause is not the lack of intelligence but the lack of resolution and courage to use it without another's guidance. *Sapere aude!* Dare to use your own intelligence! That is the motto of the Enlightenment" Quoted by Hans Kohn, *The Idea of Nationalism,* p. 397).

The Enlightenment thus began as an attempt to substitute the individual human mind as a guide to salvation, in place of the religious tradition which was mediated by sacred writings, and which was interpreted by ordained authorities. This version of the Enlightenment is generally traced to the direction which Locke gave to the conception of the human mind. His influence upon revolutionary French thought during the 18th century is unmistakable. The corollary which Locke drew from his rationalist approach to the human mind was that the separation of mankind into national societies was "conditioned by man's evil nature" (*Ibid.*, page 641, note 19).

This rational expression of the Enlightenment soon gave way to romanticism which subordinated reason itself to the dictates of the emotions. Among the most powerful and decisive emotions are those which have to do with the individual's biological survival. The society, which begins with one's own family and extends in concentric circles to the limits of one's people, comes to claim primacy, from the standpoint of life's values, rights and duties. Thus the romantic aspect of the Enlightenment, reenforced by local, economic, and political interests, nullified all traces of the cosmopolitanism which had resulted from its rational aspect, and accentuated the particularist character of the new nationalism. That particularist character, in turn, gave rise to the xenophobia that was soon to find expression in anti-Semitism.

V

The era of militant Jewish Enlightenment or *Haskala* is usually regarded as having begun with Mendelssohn. His main interest, however, was to eliminate from Jewish life what he regarded as excrescences, growing out of enforced segregation. He hoped thereby to remove the main obstacle to the civil emancipation of the Jews. He was accorded a welcome in the highest German intellectual and social circles in Berlin because of his great literary and philosophic attainments. That must have led him to assume that, if the Jews would give up the German-Jewish dialect which they had developed and instead learn to use the German of their neighbors, they would themselves pave the way for the removal of all medieval disabilities. His main concern was not with the future of the Jewish People, but with the welfare of Jews as individuals.

However, the Jewish literati whom Mendelssohn gathered
about himself, and who established the first Hebrew magazine,
known as *Ha-Meassef,* had a deep concern for the inner development of Jewish life. They were interested in having the Jews
retain their Jewish individuality, while exchanging Yiddish for
standard German. They felt that the only way to effect that purpose was through the renaissance of the Hebrew language and
the creation of a modern Hebraic literature. Those of them who
collaborated with Mendelssohn in the translation of the Bible
were eager to revive the knowledge of what they considered pure
Hebrew. Those who possessed creative literary ability deemed it
their task to revive interest in the Jewish past, particularly the
biblical era, by drawing on the Bible for their themes in prose
or poetry.

The *Haskala,* or Enlightenment movement, for a long time
encountered the bitter resistance of the Jews of Eastern Europe.
They sensed the danger to Jewish survival in the adoption of the
non-Jewish vernaculars and in the preoccupation with secular
knowledge at the expense of the Jewish studies. The diversion
from the study of Torah, they maintained, could only lead to
dejudaization and to the forefeiture of salvation in the world to
come. A wave of inter-marriage and conversion to Christianity,
they felt, was the inevitable outcome of this process of dejudaization.

It required considerable moral courage for any Jew, in that
environment, to brave the wrath of his fellow-Jews and continue
the pursuit of secular culture. While bitter opposition to secular
culture was shared by both the *Misnagdim* and the *Hasidim,* the
latter were more fanatical in their persecution of those who dared
to display an interest in secular studies. In a sense, Hasidism
became less a protest against the dry intellectualism of the *Misnagdim* than a counter-movement to the *Haskala* or Enlightenment. Despite strong opposition, however, the *Haskala* movement
continued to make headway.

The aim of the *Maskilim* who were loyal to the Jewish People
was a three-fold one: first, to win full civil rights for the Jews,
secondly, to make the Jewish masses more productive economically

and to raise their standard of living, and thirdly, to bring about a Hebraic renaissance that would inspire the Jews to take their place as a nation among the enlightened modern nations of the world. Though it would be untrue to speak of *Haskala* as deliberately aiming to turn culture into a substitute for religion, it certainly engrossed the minds of its devotees sufficiently to crowd conventional religion out of their lives.

An integral part of the Enlightenment movement was the drive to discard the artificialities of civilization and return to the simple ways of those living close to nature. That aspect of Enlightenment was not long in finding its way into the writings of the *Maskilim. Haskala* literature of that time would use, as the common setting of its subject-matter, some natural landscape as a background for labor and simple life. Shalom Hakohen, in *Mattaé Kedem al Admat Tzafon,* and Judah Leib Gordon, in *David U-Barzilai,* used the same motif. Thomas Mann has one of his characters in *Dr. Faustus* satirize the return to nature as merely having inspired a sentimental pastoral play. To which the main character replies: "Out of the pastoral play came the French Revolution."

A far more significant response to the call "Back to nature!" was the growing discontent of Jews with the rootless and haphazard character of their livelihoods, and the yearning for a productive economy, particularly agricultural. That response was not confined to those who had come under the influence of *Haskala.* Not only in East Europe, but also in the very heart of the Old City of Jerusalem where Jews were completely immune to the cultural expression of naturism, there awoke the ambition to buy land and cultivate it, and thus earn their livelihood by the sweat of their brow. That marked the beginning of the secularization of Jewish life, or the effort to change the existing environment as a means of bettering the human lot.

When, many decades later, Zionism appeared on the scene, it still had some of the original *Haskala* enthusiasm for the return to nature. Leo Pinsker, in his opening address at the Kattowitz Conference (November 6, 1885), said: "If previously we were the vehicle of traffic between man and man, we are now return-

ing to Mother Nature who gratefully blesses the hands that cultivate her, and knows no other difference among men but that of
spirit." Chasanov, one of the *Biluim* (the first wave of immigration
to Eretz Yisrael), addressed his fellow pioneers in words that
sounded "the key-note in the reconstruction of their People and
their land" as follows: "Farmer! be a free man among men, but
a slave to the soil. Kneel and bow down to it every day. Nurse
its furrows—and then even its stony clods will yield a blessing"
(Samuel Kurland, *Cooperative Palestine,* p. 6). Aaron David Gordon regarded the yearning to return to nature as the basic *motif*
of the return to Eretz Yisrael. He considered the cultivation of the
soil through labor indispensable to the rise of the new creative
type of Jew. "We have sinned through not working," writes
Joseph Chaim Brenner, the major literary exponent of the Poale
Zion—The Workers of Zion—"there is no atonement except
through labor" (*Mikan Umikan*).

VI

Insofar as *Haskala* agitated for the re-nationalization of the
Jewish People it prepared the way for the Zionist movement. The
protagonists of *Haskala* were well aware that the Jews, who had
always regarded themselves as a nation, had been treated as such
by the rest ⌐' the world. But they also sensed the difference between the kind of nation that the Jews had constituted in the
past and the kind of nation that they would have to constitute in
the future. They derived inspiration from the national movements
in 19th century Europe, in wishing to see the Jewish People take
its place among the newly born nations, as a nation dominated
by hopes and ideals which can find their fulfillment through human
endeavor amid the natural conditions in this world.

In *Or Lintivah,* the introduction to the commentary on the
Pentateuch, the first publication of Mendelssohn's collaborators
on that work, the revival of the Hebrew language is stressed as
a means to the national restoration of the Jews. One of them,
Satanov, in his *Sefer Ha-Middot* describes Eretz Yisrael as the
land where Jews will revive the Hebrew language, adopt Hebrew
personal names, etc.

To realize how far the modern national resurgence contributed to a similar awakening among East European Jews and intensified their yearning to return to Eretz Yisrael, it is necessary to recall what happened during the first part of the nineteenth century in Europe. That is concisely summed up by Carlton J. H. Hayes, an authority on the development of modern nationalism, as follows:

"Old nationalities which had long been subject to the rule of alien nationalities were induced to struggle both for political liberty and for national independence. Nationalities which had long been broken into political fragments were moved to seek national unity and national democracy. Nationalities which had been burdened by monarchical despotism were prevailed upon to revolt and to set up a democratic government which would be more intensely national. In the 1820's appeared in Europe the embryonic national states of Greece and Serbia, and in America a group of Spanish-speaking republics. In 1830 the Belgians successfully freed themselves from Dutch sovereignty, whilst the Poles unsuccessfully rebelled against Russia, and the Italians against Austria. In the 1840's, the Germans attempted to erect a democratic national state. In the 1850's and 1860's the Italians and the Rumanians alike established their national independence" (*Essays on Nationalism,* p. 57).

The Italian *risorgimento* (1815-1866) inspired the Italian people with the ideal of national renaissance and the fulfillment of Dante's loftiest dreams. Likewise the example of Germany, during the half-century prior to the proclamation of the Second Empire at Versailles, served as an incentive to the awakening of the national spirit among Jews. In Fichte's *Addresses to the German Nation* the spirit of modern nationalism attained probably its most self-conscious glorification.

In appealing for the reclamation of the soil of Eretz Yisrael through manual labor, Rabbi Zvi Hirsch Kalischer (in 1862) wrote: "That would raise our prestige in the eyes of the nations. They would say that the Jews too are people that have the urge to reclaim and renew their ancestral land. . . Why do the Italians and other peoples sacrifice their lives for their native lands? Should we not do likewise for our land which all the inhabitants of the world regard as holy, and not evade our duty like weaklings and cowards?" (*Derishat Tzion*, Warsaw, Third Edition, 1899, p. 12)

The influence of Herder and Schlegel had much to do with the Hebrew literary renaissance as an expression of modern Jewish nationhood. Toward the end of the eighteenth century, Herder wrote: "Has a people anything dearer than the speech of its fathers? In its speech resides its whole thought domain, its tradition, history, religion and basis of life, all its heart and soul." In 1812 Schlegel declared: "Every important and independent nation has a right of possessing a literature peculiar to itself. . . . It is mere prejudice which leads us to consider languages which have been neglected, or that are unknown to ourselves, as incapable of being brought to a higher perfection" (both passages quoted by Hayes in *Essays on Nationalism,* pp. 54-55).

"The doctrine of nationalism," adds Carlton Hayes, "was primarily the work of intellectuals—of scholars and literateurs. But it was more than a closet philosophy for intellectuals. It was for classes and masses" (*Ib*. p. 69).

Under the influence of Enlightenment and nationalism, *Haskala* laid the foundation of modern Jewish cultural autonomy. It sought an outlet in a cultural expression of Jewish nationhood, long before it was able to find a political outlet. The various reforms in traditional Jewish law, urged by Peretz Smolenskin and Moshe Lilienblum, were dictated by practical considerations. They steered clear of questions concerning the traditional supernatural sanctions of Jewish law. In a modern national renaissance, such as they sought to effect, there was as much need for transferring all civil law from the domain of the sacred to the domain of the secular as there was for similarly transferring the Hebrew language. Likewise the traditional legalistic approach to ritual practices was incompatible with the underlying principles of Enlightenment. Yet, no attempt was made to grapple with such basic problems. The religion of the *Maskilim* was merely modern nationalism "touched with emotion."

The Hebrew language and literature were expected to compensate for the dejudaizing influence of the awaited Emancipation and of the acquired Enlightenment. Even Judah Leib Gordon, with his motto "Be a Jew in your tent, and a man abroad," was a nationalist and not an assimilationist. That motto occurs in the poem "Awake, My People!" which was known as the Hebrew *Marseillaise*.

The purely nationalist aspect of *Haskala* influenced also traditionalist rabbis like Zvi Hirsch Kalischer, Samuel Mohilever, Judah Alkalai, Yitzhak Reiness, and a rabbinical scholar like Yehiel Michael Pines. They sought and found numerous sanctions in tradition for the need of performing mundane tasks, economically and nationally, as a means to a fuller Torah life than is possible outside Eretz Yisrael. They, too, helped to make the masses of East European Jewry responsive to political Zionism, which found but few followers among West European Jews.

VII

With the growth of anti-Semitism in Central Europe, and the tragic denouement of the Jewish struggle for emancipation, *Haskala* evolved from a cultural to a political renaissance, finally crystallizing in the movement of *Hibbat Tzion*.

In 1882 Leo Pinsker published his brochure, *Auto-Emancipation, Admonition to His Brethren by a Russian Jew*. He urged that Jews achieve a national consciousness, and exercise nationhood by acquiring a territory where they might maintain an economy and polity of their own. Both Peretz Smolenskin and Moshe Leib Lilienblum, who started out in life as *Maskilim* or "Enlighteners," finally came to the conclusion that settlement in Palestine was the only solution of the Jewish problem. To Smolenskin the *bête noire* was the Reform movement which its basic assumption that the Jews have ceased to be a nation and have become a religious community. Lilienblum was interested at first in reforming Jewish ritual practice. For a time he lost interest in Judaism altogether, and devoted himself to general studies. He became completely disoriented as a result, but finally discovered

the *Hibbat Tzion* movement, through which he found himself
again. Later he adopted the program of Herzl's political Zionism.

Even the nationalist *Maskilim,* who vacillated for a long time
in their attitude toward the idea of a return to Eretz Yisrael,
were finally won over. Nahum Sokolow, the publicist and editor
of the Warsaw Hebrew periodical *Hatzefirah,* whose Jewish nationalism was at first of the purely cultural type, later became one
of the pillars of political Zionism. Even the sceptically minded
poet, Judah Leib Gordon, admitted toward the end of his life
that secretly he had always harbored a love for Zion. Before long,
associations began to be formed in many communities of Eastern
Europe by the name of *Hovevei Tzion,* to proceed with the practical effort of establishing colonies in Palestine.

In 1896, Theodor Herzl published *The Jewish State: An
Attempt at a Modern Solution of the Jewish Question.* He emphasized the need for world recognition of the nationhood of the
Jews. "It (the Jewish question) is a national question," he wrote,
"which can be solved only by making it a political world-question
to be discussed and settled by the civilized nations of the world
in council."

Political Zionism, as promulgated by Herzl, could have made
no headway, if Jews had not been prepared for it by the *Haskala*
movement. Jews by and large had to be weaned away by *Haskala*
from their traditional supernaturalism and other-worldliness before
they were ready to listen to Herzl. In discussing the possible restoration of Eretz Yisrael to the Jews, Mendelssohn had written
that it could come about only as a result of an international war.
"The Jewish people," he stated, "due to its depressed condition
had lost its vigor. Instead of direct action, it must resort to
prayer" (*Schriften,* Volume V, p. 494). Lacking that *Haskala*
preparation in 1825, when Mordecai Noah published his proclamation inviting Jews to settle in what was to be the Jewish state
of Ararat, they laughed Noah out of court. Herzl would, no doubt,
have had the same kind of reception had he come *then* to the
Jews with his proposal to reclaim Palestine as a Jewish homeland.
They would have replied to him what they had replied to Mordecai Noah: "The redemption of the Jewish people is God's
business, not man's."

There is an even more striking proof of how the lack of proper mental conditioning, such as the *Haskala* movement provided the Jews of Central and Eastern Europe, made them deaf to the most passionate appeals and unresponsive to the most carefully formulated plans of action in behalf of a return to Eretz Yisrael. In 1861, Rabbi Alkalai Judah ben Solomon Hai, of the Croatian town of Zemlin, published among his numerous pamphlets urging a return to Eretz Yisrael, one entitled *"Shema Yisrael."* He pointed out the futility of depending upon charity for the colonization of Eretz Yisrael. The only way to achieve that purpose, he pleaded, was to have a national organization that would establish a loan bank for the development of industry, agriculture and transport, and that would negotiate with the various European governments and with the Sultan for the purchase of Eretz Yisrael. Herzl was certainly not more practical. But where Herzl succeeded, Alkalai failed. The reason was that Alkalai found the Jews of his day intellectually and spiritually unprepared. That can be seen from the way he had to plead with them: "Those who make a pretense of piety," he wrote, "by discouraging physical labor, the various skills, and the cultivation of foreign languages and assert emphatically that Jerusalem was meant to be only a place for the study of Torah are committing a sin, because *it is impossible in this world to behave as though we were in the next world, where there is no eating or drinking.*"

Political Zionism which Herzl promulgated gave to the age-old yearning of the Jews to return to Eretz Yisrael the stamp of a modern this-worldly nationalist movement. In contrast with the Emancipation to which the Jews looked forward as a concession to be granted by each country separately to its own Jews only, Zionism was presented as a claim on behalf of all Jews upon all the nations simultaneously. That is the significance of the phrase in the Basle Platform which speaks of a "publicly, legally recognized home in Palestine." The claim is presented as one that arises from the history of a People, a history which is recognized as endowing all human life with meaning. The claim, as Max Nordau pointed out in his matchless orations at one Congress after another, is backed by the duty of Western mankind to make amends for the injustices and cruelties committed against that People. Only

Herzl's daring imagination and leadership was capable of effecting
that revolutionary change in the consciousness of the Jews and in
the conception of their public relations with the Gentile world.

That the Gentile world took Herzl's agitation for a Jewish
home in Palestine seriously, and did not treat it as the utopia of
an impractical visionary, was no accident either. In the first place,
it was in line with the nationalist trend of the time. It coincided,
moreover, with proposals that had been made independently by
various writers, missionaries, clergymen and publicists, particularly in England, whence Herzl had hoped to receive his initial
moral support. It must be remembered that by that time, with
the disintegration of the Turkish Empire, and the liberation of
the Balkan states, the future of Palestine was bound to become
an object of speculation. The recollection of how Napoleon I had
contemplated settling the Jews in Palestine, as soon as he could
wrest it from the Turks, must also have lingered on. During the
latter part of the nineteenth century the European governments
were looking forward to the time when Turkey would become
spoil to be divided. The question would then arise: What will
become of Palestine? No wonder many an influential non-Jew
turned a listening ear, even if he appeared to pay no attention,
to Herzl's plea in behalf of the Jews.

*That the Jews could take Herzl seriously with his call to
return to Zion, though that call had in it nothing of the messianic
mystique, and that they had the courage to appeal to the rest of
the world for public recognition of their right to nationhood in
their ancient homeland, means that they had acquired a new
frame of mind, a new conception of themselves, of their history
and their destiny as a People.* On the one hand, it means that the
Jews became imbued with a conscious will to maintain their continuity with the People that had produced the Bible and that had
managed to survive the long precarious exile. On the other hand,
it means that the Jewish People was still sufficiently alive to want
to find a place for itself in the new world into which it had been
suddenly catapulted while yearning for a normal life like all other
peoples. The Jews were loyal to their spiritual heritage, and yet
prepared to surrender some of their most cherished beliefs. They

renounced the passive and resigned waiting for a miracle messiah and adopted the activist role of modern man. They realized that they had to take all manner of practical action before they could proceed with cultivation of the finer things in life.

Thus the Jews themselves not only reaffirmed their nation-hood but also proved their willingness to incorporate it in a state. That was a prerequisite to world recognition as a nation. That was the main function of the World Zionist Congress which had its first session in Basle, and which adopted the following Platform:

"The aim of Zionism is to create for the Jewish People a publicly recognized, legally secured Home in Palestine.

"In order to attain this object the Congress adopted the following measures:

1. To promote the settlement in Palestine of Jewish agriculturists, handicraftsmen, industrialists and men following professions.

2. To centralize the Jewish People by means of general institutions conformable to the laws of the land.

3. To strengthen Jewish sentiment and national self-consciousness.

4. To obtain the sanctions of government necessary for carrying out the objects of Zionism."

Originally Herzl hoped that the wealthy Jews of the West would finance the migration of Central and East European Jews to Palestine. Only when he failed to meet with an encouraging response in Paris and London did he awake to the fact that Jewish self-emancipation means personal commitment to the idea of settling in Eretz Yisrael. Such commitment could only come from East European Jews who, on the one hand, had outgrown the psychology of passive endurance of Jewish disabilities and, on the other hand, had culturally become obsessed with the hope of a return to Zion.

The well known publicist Israel Cohen of England reminisced recently about Herzl. "The first time when I saw Herzl," he writes, "was at the first public meeting that he addressed in London. The reason he decided to speak at this meeting was because the exposition of his ideas to the members of the Maccabean Club, a gathering of intellectuals, had met with a lukewarm reception. As he failed with the élite of London Jewry, he was resolved to win over the masses. . . . The great majority of the audience were natives of Russia, some of whom had come to England only recently and others some years previously, though all alike had had vivid memories of the Tsarist persecutions from which they had fled" (*Opinion*, July-August 1954).

Though Herzl's political Zionism would have fallen on arid soil had that soil not been plowed up by *Haskala* and cultural Zionism, it is equally true that without political Zionism the impact of cultural Zionism would soon have spent itself. A culture cannot thrive long on memories and dreams.

"There is no doubt," we are told in a statement that appeared in 1939 immediately after the issuance of the White Paper, "that the authors of the Mandate for Palestine hoped to found a Jewish State in Palestine, and the principal reason why that was not declared unambiguously as their object was that in 1917 no one could know for certain how great the response of the Jews would be. . ." (*Palestine*, Organ of the British Palestine Committee, May 24, 1939).

VIII

What political Zionism has contributed to the evolution of Judaism can be properly evaluated only when we understand the significance of Herzl's mission and of the Zionist World Organization which he established. That significance is aptly set forth in the distinction drawn by Marvin Lowenthal between Herzl and the pseudo-messiahs like Moses of Crete, David Alroy, Abraham Abulafia, Solomon Molko and Sabbatai Zevi. "The messianic pretenders," he says "obeyed a stock idea which they had neither created nor modified, and their careers added to Jewish life nothing real or ideal, not even a salutary disappointment. They came to fulfill a hope which floundered as well, or better, without them, and they departed without advancing, or more happily, retarding their cause.

"Herzl was likewise a servant of his days and its peculiar ideals. But there the resemblance ends. For he was not merely obedient to the current ideals of nationalism; he was largely their sponsor in Jewish life. And he not only sponsored them, but, absorbing them for the greater part without the main stream of Jewish life, he succeeded in imposing them on the Jewish world. This imposition was his first heroic achievement.

"The expectation of a messiah which gave the first eighteen centuries of exile a purpose finally dwindled to a mumbled phrase in the mouths of a mumbling people. Herzl broke the lethargy of an age, and his figure glows in consequence with the heroic light of a folklore prince.

"The Zionist Organization is more than an organization, it is a Church, a social movement, an intangible State, a far flung permeating body of energy and ideas. Both in the opposition provoked and the complementary forces it set in motion, it altered and continues to alter Jewish life. No community is so removed, or *hevra* so minute, as to go untouched. Countless and incredibly devious efforts, from the *Menorah Journal* to the settlements in Crimea, have arisen, sometimes willy and sometimes nilly, from this institution which is the lengthened shadow of one man.

"Herzl was the first Jew to attempt to abolish the economic misery of the masses through an appeal to the Jewish spirit, and to remove the burden of moral suffering through political action. It means Herzl thought in terms of high finance and world politics instead of cultural and religious mysticism" (Marvin Lowenthal, *Menorah Journal,* Volume XV, p. 320).

Both Pinsker and Herzl constituted a challenge to cultural Zionism to awaken in modern minded Jews the will to become a modern nation. That required the formulation of a philosophy of Judaism, which would appeal to the Jew to the extent of bringing new life to his moribund will to remain a Jew. The outstanding Jewish thinker who understood the challenge and who met it with remarkable clarity of thought and consuming zeal was Ahad Ha'am. He was the first to take fully into account the change from a supernaturalistic and other-worldly to a nationalistic and this-worldly climate of opinion, and to stress the need

of preparing the Jews and Judaism for national rebirth. He was
the first to realize the correlation between Zionism and Judaism,
and to recognize that *only the desire for a rebirth of Judaism can
give rise to the right kind of Zionism.* Ahad Ha'am conceived
that rebirth as a revival of prophetic Judaism, which to him meant
the drive toward an order of society based on justice. He deprecated the traditional emphasis on other-worldliness, mainly because
it stressed individual, at the expense of national, salvation.

Later, Buber, who had been influenced by Ahad Ha'am's call
for spiritual preparedness as a prerequisite to national revival,
stressed the need of having preparedness take on a more personal
form, which could find expression in a deepened God-consciousness. He assumed that Jewish hereditary traits warranted the
expectation that a return to their land would bring them to
spiritual eminence. He stressed the need for the emergence of a
new type of Jewish person, and played down the importance of
a collective consciousness.

Ber Borochov and Nachman Syrkin stressed the translation
of this-worldliness into economic justice, which they identified with
socialism, the former on Marxist grounds, the latter on ethical
grounds. Berditchevski urged a Nietzschean transvaluation; the
sovereignty of the individual and the primacy of the will to power
as man's basic drive.

Pre-State Zionism was thus the outgrowth of the meeting of
cultural or *Haskala* Zionism with political Zionism. *Haskala* Zionism was evolved among East European Jews who, never having
enjoyed the benefits of complete emancipation, had always looked
forward to it, but who finally became convinced that it would
never materialize. Though, for the most part, fostered by lay
scholars and writers, *Haskala* Zionism was also adopted by a number of rabbis who regarded worldly culture and pursuits as essential
to normal Jewish life.

On the other hand, nothing much would have happened
without political Zionism. In adopting the goal of an internationally
recognized home for Jewry, Zionism took the one step that might
ultimately eradicate from the minds of the Gentile world the biases
based upon its mystical conception of Jews and Judaism and

replace those biases with something like a sympathetic understanding. Psychologically, people are what they feel, think, and do, when they react to what others think of them. With the confused idea that the Gentile world has of us Jews, it is almost inevitable that we should react incoherently. To establish a concrete and desirable image of ourselves in the minds of others is all essential. That is what only political Zionism could accomplish. The significance of this achievement is crudely expressed in the feeling that the attainment of Zionist purpose would raise Jewish self-respect and the respect of the rest of the world for the Jews.

From the standpoint of naturalistic this-worldly salvation, the basis of Jewish unity can no longer be merely a tradition which served mainly to qualify all who lived by it for bliss in the hereafter. What Jews need now is living collective experience that they can share in common. Due to the destruction of autonomous communal life and the disintegrative influence of the Emancipation, that common experience has had to be found in the chronic plague of anti-Semitism. Political Zionism, on the other hand, has provided such collective experience in the common task which now devolves upon world Jewry: to consolidate the State of Israel and to make it the home of Jewish civilization.

In sum, the Zionist movement could have come into being only as a result of the intellectual and spiritual preparation which Jews had received through the *Haskalah* movement, with its initial efforts to transform the other-worldly outlook and way of life of the Jewish people. *The Zionist movement is thus not merely the outcome of the need of Jews for a haven of refuge from persecution or discrimination. It is principally a response of the Jewish People to its inner drive to metamorphose itself into a new corporate entity, by transposing its spiritual heritage into the key of naturalistic and this-worldly salvation.* "There is at bottom only one problem in the world, and this is its name," writes Thomas Mann, "How does one burst the cocoon and become a butterfly?" (*Dr. Faustus,* Chapter XXX, page 308).

BIBLIOGRAPHY

BER BOROCHOV, *Nationalism and the Class Struggle*, N. Y., Poale Zion of America, 1937.

ISRAEL COHEN, *The Zionist Movement*, N. Y., Zionist Organization of America, 1946.

THEODOR HERZL, *The Jewish State*, N. Y., American Zionist Emergency Council, 1946.

LEON SIMON, *Selected Essays by Ahad Ha'am*, Phila., Jewish Publication Society, 1912.

SHALOM SPIEGEL, *Hebrew Reborn*, N. Y., Macmillan, 1930.

MEYER WAXMAN, *A History of Jewish Literature*, N. Y., Bloch Publishing Co., 1936, Vol. III, Chs. 2-10; Vol. IV, Ch. 12.

——. *Rome and Jerusalem*, MOSES HESS, N. Y., Bloch Publishing Co.

CHAPTER III

The Perspective of
Pre-State Zionism

I

CULTURAL ZIONISM, which evolved out of the *Haskala* movement in the East European countries, aimed at nothing less than the reconstruction of the inner as well as the outer life of the Jewish People. It intended not only to redeem the Jewish People, but also to regenerate its spirit. Had *Haskala* been permitted to work itself out over a longer period of time, East European Jewry might have been able to negotiate the transition from other-worldly to this-worldly Judaism. But it was assailed by the two extremes of assimilationism and intransigeant fanaticism. Being attacked on the front and in the rear, it was unable to marshall its forces and conduct an orderly campaign in its struggle for Jewish survival. Its own shortcomings were carried over into pre-State Zionism, a synthesis of cultural with political Zionism, which was too engrossed in urgent problems to see Jewish life steadily and whole.

Pre-State Zionism was inherently incapable of coping with the Jewish problem of world Jewry as a whole. Its outlook was limited to perspectives of the nineteenth century European environment in which it arose. The world in which pre-State Zionism originated was one where feudalism and clericalism were well on the way to being replaced by a civilization nationalist in form, egalitarian in content, and naturalist in outlook. Such a civilization was inherently this-worldly in orientation. But the inertia of centuries could not be easily overcome. Hence the inner contradictions that still beset Western civilization as a whole, contradictions which have made it difficult for Jews to arrive at a consistent policy in ordering their own lives and in the reconstruction of their People's destiny.

As we look back to pre-State Zionism, we cannot help noting that it was largely derivative and defensive rather than creative in character. "It is not from Jewish life," confessed Ber Borochov, the philosopher of the *Poale Zion* movement, "that we derive our socialism, radicalism, liberalism and clericalism. Our differing social ideologies are mere reflections of the life of our neighbors" (*Nationalism and the Class Struggle*, p. 96).

Zionism was defensive in its response to the growing threat of the extermination of the Jews of Europe, and also derivative in aspiring to a Jewish future defined by the values and ideals which contributed so largely to that very danger. Nationalism, socialism and materialistic empiricism conspired to make the position of the Jews in Europe untenable; yet they were accepted by leading *Maskilim* and Zionists as the ultimate values of civilization. It did not occur to them that, while a shift from other-worldliness to this-worldliness was inevitable, that change did not necessarily have to take a form which demanded a complete break with Jewish tradition. The possibility that nationalism might give birth to chauvinism, that socialism might lead to totalitarian despotism, or that materialistic empiricism was fatal to any national renaissance, never suggested itself to the architects of pre-State Zionism. They adopted the three prevalent modern trends without discrimination, without attempting to isolate those elements of permanent and universal value which could serve as a challenge enlarging the horizons of Jewish tradition.

Pre-State Zionism, with its limited perspective, generally assumed—and in certain quarters, particularly in Israel, the assumption still prevails—that nothing less that a total exodus to Eretz Yisrael was necessary for the survival of the Jewish People. European Zionists failed to realize the extent to which Jews were psychologically unprepared for the kind of nationalist drive essential to such an exodus. The notable exception was Ahad Ha'am. His recognition of the lack of a national will among the Jews, his clear understanding of the reason for this condition and his insistence that it must be remedied, distinguished him from other leaders of the Zionist movement both before and after Herzl. When Herzl said: "If you will it, it need be no legend," he had no conception of the transformation Jews had to undergo, before they could acquire the will to return to their ancient homeland.

Even Ahad Ha'am was convinced that it was impossible for Judaism to take root in the Diaspora. His assumption that Eretz Yisrael would serve as a spiritual center sustaining Jewish life in the Diaspora referred to a transitional period preparatory to the ultimate ingathering of all Jews to Zion. It is true that he expected that interim period to last a long time. He did not expect the Jews to be fully prepared for national autonomy before a number of generations had passed. But that a permanent Diaspora could be part of the destiny of the Jewish People never entered his mind.

After Herzl's death, when the Zionist movement suffered a kind of suspended animation, because all roads to the realization of its political goal seemed closed, Ahad Ha'amism came into its own. It was translated into an elaborate system of Hebrew education and communal organization. The underlying *motif* in this intensified Zionism in Eastern Europe was *hakhshara,* or physical and mental preparation for life in Eretz Yisrael. In the spirit of Ahad Ha'am's teaching, part of that *motif* was to create *discontent* with existence in the Diaspora, even under the most favorable political and civic conditions. What was the effect of all that preparation for Eretz Yisrael and of *discontent* with Diaspora? One of the outstanding negators of Diaspora concedes that "no Zionist mass departure was produced by this state of mind" (Simon Halkin, "Zionism and the State of Israel" in *Forum,* Dec. 1953).

That the limited perspective of pre-State Zionism still prevails can be seen from Zionist spokesmen in Israel. Referring to the need of improving the situation in American Zionism, Halkin writes: "That improvement means a realization that Jewish life can be lived to the full only by proceeding to Eretz Yisrael, and, at the least, educating one's children to the necessity of proceeding there and striking root there in due course."

For the Jews to leave the countries of the Diaspora, one of the following conditions would have to obtain: (1) in the case of those living completely within the limits of the traditional universe of thought, and totally impervious to alternative cultural

influences, they would have to believe in the call to return to Eretz
Yisrael as emanating directly from God; or (2) in the case of
those living within a modern, this-worldly universe of thought, they
would have to be so persecuted in the countries of the Diaspora as
to find life intolerable there.

If neither of the foregoing conditions obtained, the possibility
of a large exodus is out of the question. A third alternative is
migration of a sufficient number to consolidate the State and the
permanent existence of a Diaspora Jewry. This third alternative,
however, has never been considered by the architects of pre-State
Zionism for the following reasons:

A. They could not imagine that the Jewish religion might
be so transformed through the establishment of a Jewish homeland as to become compatible with the modern universe of thought,
and fit to serve as a bond of unity between Eretz Yisrael and the
Diaspora.

B. They regarded socialism as an adequate substitute for
traditional Jewish religion and as capable of satisfying the ethical
impulse inherent in the Jewish People.

C. They could not conceive of any country outside a Jewish
homeland so free from anti-Semitism as to render Jewish life not
only tolerable but satisfying.

Those are the reasons why it never occurred to the architects
of pre-State Zionism to plan a mode of life for those Jews who,
with all that they might do politically and financially to help in
the establishment of a Jewish homeland, would not think of going
there to live. They failed to translate Zionism into a personal and
communal program of Jewish life for Diaspora Jewry. That failure
is responsible for the turn which Zionism took in America. It
became a purely philanthropic movement. Even its severest critics
must admit that, without philanthropic Zionism, the State of Israel
could not have come into being. Yet, failing a Zionist philosophy
that could make a difference in the personal and communal life
of Diaspora Jewry, the steadily widening cultural and spiritual
gap between the Jews in Israel and the rest of world Jewry is
leading both groups from frustration to frustration

A.

With the exception of Buber, most of the thinkers including Ahad Ha'am developed a definitely secular conception of Jewish nationalism, which was, at best, to find collective expression in some ethical or social system of values. Though these secularist thinkers would have been the first to deplore conversion to a non-Jewish religion as apostasy, they never took the trouble to explain why, on the one hand, they relegated religion to the private discretion, or conscience, of the individual, and on the other, condemned him, if he used that right to become a Christian or a Moslem.

The cavalier fashion in which religion was dismissed from pre-State ideology can not only be explained, but, to a large extent, also excused. The bitter experiences of those who attempted to tamper with established creed or ritual in Eastern Europe left certain ineradicable prejudices and blind spots which have made it impossible for the Zionist leaders to deal objectively with the problem of religion and its place in Jewish life, either in Israel or in the Diaspora. The tendency of religious leaders "to cooperate with the ruling classes and their vested interests both in a spiritual and in a material sense" (Karl Mannheim, *The Diagnosis of Our Time*, p. 110), so prevalent on the Continent, was as evident among Jews as it was among Christians. Moreover, the human frailties and aggressions exhibited by the various churches in Christianity, the intransigeance of the Roman Catholic, the Greek Orthodox, and the Fundamentalist and Evangelical Protestant clerics, their insistence upon the surrender of intellectual and personal freedom to ecclesiastical authority and their hostility to all moral and spiritual progress, persuaded Jews, harassed by their own religious and lay leaders, that religion held no hope whatever for improving the material or spiritual condition of the Jewish People.

An additional factor reinforced the tendency to ignore the problem of religion. In the countries where Jews were emancipated, the religious congregations, other than those established by recent immigrants from Eastern Europe, at first deliberately sought to obstruct and sabotage the Zionist movement. The *Protest-*

rabbiner, among whom were outstanding rabbis of Western Judaism, blocked permission by the Munich municipality for the first Zionist Congress to convene in that city. When Herzl came for the first time to London, Sir Samuel Montagu, who was President of the Federation of Synagogues, refused to chair the public meeting at which Herzl was to present the case for Zionism. His son, equally well known as a synagogue Jew, fought hard to prevent the issuance of the Balfour Declaration, and Rabbi Isaac M. Wise in America ridiculed Zionism as a wild adventure, calling it "Ziomania."

No wonder, therefore, that the Zionist movement as a whole gave Jewish religion a wide berth. The Mizrahi wing, with its intransigeant orthodoxy, only strengthened the tendency of the main Zionist leadership to dismiss the entire problem of religion. But, though it may have been possible for the Zionist movement to advance towards its immediate objective—the establishment of a state—without considering the problem of Jewish religion, that is no longer the case. *It has become imperative to overcome the deep prejudices against religion generated by the past behavior of religionists.* That behavior was the outcome of a long history of ignorance, superstition and narrow-mindedness shared by all peoples and civilizations. Enlightenment should enable us to distinguish between those elements in religious behavior which retard man's development and those which lead on to maturity.

The elements in religious behavior which have alienated Zionists are deeply rooted in the popular mind, but they are by no means an essential part of religion. They can be unlearned, and are actually being unlearned. Eliminating them will give rise to a more moral and spiritual religion, in keeping with the cultural and social development of modern civilizations.

The assumptions concerning religion which have proved a stumbling block to Zionist thinking are the following:

(a) The only genuine kind of religion is that which is based on supernaturalism and is other-worldly and eschatological (pertaining to "last things") in its outlook.

(b) Ritual and institutional practices constitute the main content of religion.

(c) Since it is the purpose of religion to identify and conserve the absolute and the unchanging, religion is inherently incapable of responding to the needs of a dynamic age like ours.

(d) Religion inherently requires a group that not only specializes in matters of moral and spiritual concern, but also has the authority to compel obedience to its teachings and decrees.

The fact that most peoples cannot dissociate religion from the foregoing assumptions has resulted in the situation aptly described by Aaron David Gordon. "More than religion has stagnated," he said, "the concept of religion has stagnated." Both *Haskala* and Zionism failed to reckon with "the deep interrelation between language, religion and patriotism." There can be no meaning to the life struggle of a people, unless it can evolve its own historic consciousness, and unless its history is accompanied by a religious feeling, that is, by a spiritual sensitivity which discerns in events the workings of a divine process.

"National renascence," says Franz Rosenzweig, "based on the assimilation of classical antiquity played itself out by the end of the 19th century, because the ship of Nationality hasn't enough draught to navigate the ocean of world history. It can only acquire this by placing the cargo of Christianity in its hold. Anti-Christianity might also serve, as he who opened the way to the modern epoch has shown. But indifference won't, for it leads of necessity to classicism. So all that remains to us of the ballast, if we don't want to become Christians, in our Judaism. Compared with the Christian ballast ours is a little heavy, but the ship won't sink, it moves, as I have experienced" (Glatzer, *Franz Rosenzweig,* page 136).

At the General Convention in January-February 1945 of the *Histadrut, the* "General Federation of Jewish Workers," the group calling itself "Religious Workers" was represented by only five delegates out of 423, in contrast with *Mapai,* which had 226, and the more radical socialists, who had 87. From the standpoint of ethical influence, which should be the true measure of religion, there is incomparably more of the truly religious spirit in the basic principles by which members of the *Histadrut* are expected to regulate their daily lives than in the most devout worship and

ritual practices. But in failing to recognize this, in the inability to
see those transcendental or cosmic meanings which give point to
its own ethical striving, the *Histadrut* is missing its opportunity
to make Zionism the kind of humanist religious movement that
it must become, if Zionism is to survive. That attitude on the
part of the most important creative element of the Jews in Israel
is largely the consequence of the narrow empiricism within which
Karl Marx confined all human values.

In view of the harmful effects of "the stagnation of the concept of religion," Zionist leaders and thinkers must reorient themselves with regard to religion in general and Jewish religion in
particular. At this point, it is sufficient to note that *faith in the
highest potentialities of human nature and persistence in activating
them cannot be sustained without a religious feeling for history
and the time process, or without a sense of destiny which transcends the life of individuals and societies.* It is only that kind of
religious feeling which can keep alive in us the faith that the
forces of love and of reconciliation are stronger than those of hate
and war.

It is essential, too, to be fully aware of the progress of the
human mind from the crude notions of cause and effect expressed
in magic, to our highly developed modern understanding of the
forces at work in man and his environment. The fact that the
human mind has outgrown particular ideas it had of God does
not mean that it has outgrown the need of believing in God.
Many have been the notions concerning selfhood or personality
that. have had to be outgrown, yet no one in his senses would
ever think of suggesting that we abandon the belief in the self
and renounce all personal pronouns in our thinking and com-
munication. The case with regard to the belief in God is entirely
analogous.

The fact that all progress is uneven, and that a widespread
cultural lag affects religious development, no doubt makes it difficult for people to conceive of religion as the soul of a culture
or civilization, and to understand that it must evolve in history.
When a religion is out of step with its civilization, the solution
does not lie in relegating all religious questions to the individual

preference. That might be the case with other-worldly religion, but this-worldly religion is far too intimately bound up with social relationships and activities to be treated as entirely a private affair.

Since it is not the fear of anti-Semitism, but the love of Judaism as a religious civilization, that will have to motivate Diaspora Jews in their concern for the State of Israel, it is essential to understand what changes traditional Judaism has to undergo, if it is to survive in the modern world.

B.

A second shortcoming of pre-State Zionism was the indiscriminate acceptance on the part of the leading sector within it of Marxist Socialism and the idea of class struggle as a key concept for the interpretation of history, and a method of achieving economic and social equality. Of the two, the use of the class struggle concept is far more serious. That concept nullifies the intrinsic significance of those moral and spiritual values without which Jewish tradition becomes a mere jumble of outlived beliefs and superstitious practices. The Marxian analysis portrays the Jewish People as having been tormented without purpose on the Ixion wheel of the so-called universal class struggle. Moreover, as a method for achieving a more livable social order, the theory of the class struggle reduces the struggle for any national renaissance to an absurdity. In opposing Zionism, the Marxist Jewish *Bund* in Poland was at least partially consistent. Had it yielded to Lenin's demand to disband and renounce all relationship with the Jewish People, it would have been entirely consistent.

But logic and consistency were thrown to the winds by the most constructive elements of the Second and Third waves of immigration to Eretz Yisrael. Though the cooperative method of establishing their settlements was the only one that could render them viable, in the face of the conditions with which they had to contend, they nevertheless felt it necessary to justify that method in terms of doctrinaire Socialism. Only occasionally did a wise leader know enough not to insist on doctrine. For example, at the Conference at Haifa on December 4, 1920, where the various

labor groups finally succeeded in uniting and establishing the
Histadrut (Federation of Labor), Berl Katznelson, who spoke on
behalf of the largest of the four groups represented there, said:
"A trade union, unattended by Zionism, and a sense of responsibility for building the land not combined with socialism
(though it need not bear just that name)—such a trade union
simply cannot be in Eretz Yisrael" (Kurland, *Cooperative Palestine,* p. 30). The *Poale Zion* and *The Jewish Socialist Workers'
Party* (M. P. S. I.) were uncompromisingly socialistic, the latter
even at the expense of Jewish nationalism, which they condemned
as inherently bourgeois in character. At least they were consistent
in maintaining that the class struggle was far more important than
Zionism.

This extraordinary influence of Marxist Socialism upon those
who laid the foundations of Jewish nationhood is another striking
illustration of the derivative character of pre-State Zionism, and
of its inability to overcome the variety of *Galut*-nurtured habits of
thought which the early settlers had brought with them. Like its
indifference to religion, the failure of Zionism to create its own
conception of economic and social justice, the basis for which
might well have been found in the Jewish tradition, disqualifies
pre-State Zionism as the urgently needed bond of unity between
the Jews in Israel itself, and between the Jewry of Israel and
Diaspora Jewries.

c.

A third shortcoming of pre-State Zionism, which accounts
for its inadequate conception of the future of the Diaspora, has
been its failure to comprehend the distinctive character of Anglo-
American democracy. The United States alone harbors almost six
million Jews; that is somewhat more than 50 percent of the total
Jewish population. The climate of opinion which is the product
of Anglo-American democracy, though no less this-worldly than
the European, nevertheless differs from it in being incomparably
more conducive to the security and peace of mind of Jews. Zionist
leaders should have had the foresight to note that difference and
to draw practical conclusions from it. That would have saved
the Zionist movement from its present very serious predicament,

arising from the widespread misunderstanding of the nature of the mutual relations between Israel and American Jews.

It cannot be said that the Anglo-American climate of opinion is altogether free from the nationalism, socialism and materialistic empiricism which pervade the Continental climate of opinion. But there is a tremendous difference in the way those values or ideals function here and on the Continent. That difference provides American Jews with a margin of safety which must necessarily affect their attitude toward migrating to Eretz Yisrael, and their conception of the destiny of the Jewish People.

Nationalism in the United States tends to be isolationist, instead of expansionist, as is the case in the old world. Socialism, even in Britain, takes the form of Fabianism rather than Marxism, and in the United States is replaced by the welfare state. As for materialistic empiricism, it is hardly more than a kind of esoteric cult in Anglo-American circles, instead of a thoroughgoing philosophy of life with strict application to politics and economics.

These modifications of the Continental climate of opinion are not accidental. They are traceable to the ineradicable influences of the biblical tradition, which has played a significant role in English culture and politics. Those influences have passed over into American politics and culture, as a result, at first, of the part which the Puritan, and later, the New England spirit, had in moulding the American mind. Those who originally lived by that spirit went so far as to identify themselves with the Israel of the Bible, and to transfer to their own time literally many of the forms and institutions of biblical times, all in the interest of the rights of the individual as against the power and authority of the most august collective body, be it church, nation or state.

Pre-modern Zionist thinkers and leaders concentrated their attention upon their own European environment. America did not produce a single major Zionist thinker. Hence not even the fact that, from the 80's of the last century until World War I, East European Jewish migration turned to America in vastly greater numbers than to Eretz Yisrael, opened their eyes to the need for a more comprehensive approach to the Jewish problem.

Only anti-Zionist *Maskilim,* as in the case of the poet Judah
Leib Gordon, took cognizance of the Jewish migration to America. In a poem called *Tashlik,* addressed to a friend of his who
had left for the United States, he despairs of the promised return
of the Jews to Eretz Yisrael. He tells his friend that in a mood of
bitterness in one of his earlier poems he had taken God to task
for having raised the fortunes of Spain by enabling Columbus to
discover for her a new world in the very year that she banished
her Jews. But he has since learned to know better. For, the
New World which Columbus discovered offers a haven of refuge
to the Jewish people in the United States, Argentina and Brazil.
It would be unreasonable to expect that the poet Gordon should
look beyond the opportunity which the New World offered the
Jews to live in peace, and to ask himself how long they were
likely to foster their Jewish individuality.

But those who had set their hearts on *Hibat Tzion,* and
who could see no alternative future for the Jewish people other
than migration to Eretz Yisrael, were completely oblivious to the
possibilities of the New World. That applies to an Ahad Ha'am
no less than to a Buber, to a Weizmann no less than to a Jabotinsky. All of them took it for granted that the climate of opinion
generated by Continental Europe was bound to invade the rest
of the world. They therefore inferred that the rest of the world
could not prove any more hospitable to Jewish life than the
European continent. Hence there was nothing else for Jews to
do, no matter where they lived, but to return to their ancient
home where they would be masters of their own fate.

II

As matters stand at present, it appears that Jewish survival
anywhere in the world, whether it be in Israel or outside it, is
possible only so long as the world will be safe for Anglo-American
civilization with its intrinsic spirit of democracy. That civilization
is conducive to a climate of opinion, which though this-worldly,
has highly significant points of contact with what is basic in the
Jewish tradition. In a book entitled *The Bible in America:
Versions That Have Played Their Part in the Making of the Re-*

public, Marion Simms describes the extent to which values derived from the Bible have gone into the shaping of the American conscience. That fact, though seemingly intangible, should have the effect of dispelling what we found to be the initial shock to Judaism, when after many centuries of having generated the climate of opinion by which two-thirds of mankind had lived, it suddenly discovered itself thrust into a climate of opinion that negated all of its great life values.

In the atmosphere of Anglo-American democracy, with its history and basic drive, Jews who are familiar with the prophetic strand of their own tradition have good reason to feel at home. The experience of Jews in Anglo-American countries, where democratic nationalism still obtains, warrants the expectation that Judaism can thrive there. Despite its ancillary status in a country like the United States, Judaism can evolve there a way of life that would enable the Jew to help maintain the high ideals by which the American nation strives to shape its life. "The American Idea," as Horace M. Kallen so forcefully points out, "is the national faith in democracy as the religion of religions which guarantees equal liberty to each of upward three hundred sects and denominations. It hence requires of them that they should be united in common loyalty to this democratic faith. The American Idea designs the national economy as the free coming together of men and managements in common enterprises, moved by a common concern so to raise the national standard of living that all may live their lives in ever greater abundance because of the ever widening knowledge and truer skills wherewith they earn their livings" ("Whither Israel?", *The Menorah Journal,* Vol. 39; No. 2, p. 136).

Should Anglo-American civilization, too, in its struggle against totalitarian aggression, be led to renounce the spirit of democracy and adopt the outlook and strategy of its enemy, there would be no room for Jewish group life anywhere in the world. Only on the assumption that man's love of freedom will prevent the political balance of the world from swinging to the Soviets, or that freedom will ultimately penetrate the Soviet orbit itself, can we hope for Jewish survival not only in Israel but anywhere in the world.

These considerations are entirely lacking in pre-State Zionist
ideology. It never occurred to the architects of Zionism to reckon
with a situation like that in which American Jews find themselves. Dubnow is undoubtedly correct in maintaining that "both
political and spiritual Zionism have their roots in the same common ground, in the 'negation of the Golus,' in the conviction
that outside of Palestine—in the lands of the Diaspora—the
Jewish People has no possibility of continuing its existence as
a normal national entity. Both political and spiritual Zionists have
their eyes equally fixed upon Zion as the anchor of safety for
Judaism, whether it be in its material or in its spiritual aspect.
Neither doctrine has formulated a clear idea of the future destinies
of the Jewish Diaspora, that is of the destinies of the entire Jewry
of the world, minus the section settled in Palestine" (*The Jews
in Russia and Poland,* Volume III, pp. 51-52).

Unfortunately, Dubnow himself was under the illusion that
in promulgating his "spiritual nationalism" he had formulated
"a clear idea of the future destinies of the Jewish Diaspora." He
reckoned only with the European environment prior to World
War I, when, on the basis of the complicated situation presented
by the Austrian Empire, certain political theoreticians hoped
that it would be possible to establish autonomous forms of life
for the numerous nationalities in Central and Eastern Europe by
granting them communal, cultural, educational and linguistic
minority rights. All those nationalities would lack for full nationhood would be political sovereignty. A modern state could thus
be multi-national. Dubnow proposed that the Jews should likewise lay claim to autonomous cultural and communal rights.
That would constitute their spiritual nationhood.

In invoking that parallel, Dubnow overlooked one important difference. All other national minorities that were demanding
autonomy occupied specific territories with which they were
identified. The Jews lacked that advantage; they were territorially
rootless. Had the principle of minority nationalities proved effective—as it did not—the Jews could hardly have benefited by
it, even though it was formally adopted at the Versailles Peace
Conference. Even if the principle had worked in the case of

European Jewry, it would have been entirely irrelevant to the political pattern of the United States and other countries which refuse to recognize the existence of minority nationalities.

It was common for Zionists to point to the peoples of the Austrian and Turkish Empires who achieved national independence as examples to be emulated by the Jews. They did not seem to realize the striking difference between being rooted in a land, as was the case with each of those peoples, and having to return to a land which was virtually closed, and whose Government kept those Jews who managed to enter under strict surveillance, lest they dare aspire to group autonomy. Moreover, the fact that the Jews figured in the consciousness of the rest of the world as a people closely united, though accursed and rejected by God, does not mean that Jews among themselves possessed what Renan regarded as the chief requirement of nationality—"a clearly expressed desire to live a common life."

Ahad Ha'am correctly diagnosed the psychology of the Jew. He traced to the Rabbinic version of Judaism, with its eschatological and other-worldly conception of salvation, the loss of the will to nationhood—or of "the desire to live a common life." He was well aware of the long and difficult process of reeducation needed to revive in the Jews a will to nationhood, and to let it strike roots in the common economic, social and cultural interests which only those who live in a country of their own can normally cultivate.

We can no longer operate with the limited perspective of the founders of the movement. *We have to widen the Zionist perspective so as to involve all Jews throughout the world in the upbuilding of the State of Israel, whether they expect to migrate to Eretz Yisrael or to remain permanently in the Diaspora.*

Half of world Jewry is in the United States. The State of Israel can absorb at most far below half of the present Jewish population. These facts call for a reformulation of Zionism, so that it will reckon with the conditions created for Jewish life by a this-worldly climate of opinion.

To this day, the limited perspective of Zionists leads them to rely on fear of anti-Semitism as the principal motive for migra-

tion to Israel. They can see no distinction between the American
and the European brand of anti-Semitism, except in the degree
of power to harm, a difference which they think will disappear
with time. They read into the economic discrimination that exists
in the United States, and the feeling of insecurity which attends
the economic success of Jews, a more sinister significance than
the situation warrants.

With all the insecurity to which Jews, being a minority
group, are subject, they are for a long time bound to be more
secure in the United States than they are likely to be in Israel.
Moreover, if fear of anti-Semitism is to be the motive for migrating from the United States, what is to guarantee that Jew-hatred
will not overtake them in Israel and endanger their position
vis-a-vis the Arab world ? One might have expected Max Nordau
to realize that the fate of the Jews in the United States is bound
to be different from that of the Jews in Europe. In an article
of his, which appeared in *The New York American,* July 9 and
16, 1916, entitled "America, Noah's Ark," he contrasted the
United States with the European countries, and portrayed it as
a land in which prevailed the blessings of "liberty, justice, frater-
nity, humanity, charity, respect for individual freedom . . . peace
and good will." Yet even he failed to grasp the significance of the
difference, as far as the future of American Jewry was concerned.

Maurice Samuel recently called attention to the fact that
"the re-creation of the Jewish homeland is an integral part of
the folklore of the Western world . . . There is no Russian or
Polish tradition for the creation of a Jewish state. There are no
individual Russians or Poles corresponding to a Shaftesbury, a
Balfour, a Smuts, a Sir Wyndham Deedes, to a Lodge or Wilson
or Roosevelt. There are no such figures in other former countries
of most Israelis. Hence, generally speaking, the Israelis cannot
understand why it is that American Jews have this deep attachment for America" (*Hadassah Newsletter,* March, 1954).

The American climate of opinion, despite its saturation with
ideas and values deriving from the naturalist and nationalist conceptions of reality, still retains significant ties with the Jewish

tradition. That is clearly demonstrated in the decorative map of the United States and the accompanying study, published by Lottie and Moshe Davis. The study records no less than one thousand cities and towns, throughout the country from the Atlantic to the Pacific, that bear Biblical names. Even if the significance of that fact seldom figures in the consciousness of the average citizen, the role of the Bible in forming the American mind exercises a subconscious influence and rises clearly to consciousness from time to time among those who mold opinion. There is something about the American spirit of democracy and justice which is definitely conductive to a sympathetic interest in the upbuilding of Israel. To cite one instance, there was no group of Jews more antagonistic to the Zionist movement than those immigrant workers who had come to this country from East Europe, imbued with socialist and (Jewish) Bundist prejudices. Zionism, they held, was a hobby of the Jewish bourgeoisie, and, therefore, should be resisted at all costs. Not even the Balfour Declaration was enough to overcome that prejudice. All discussion of Zionism was banned from the overwhelmingly Jewish needle trades unions. In 1923 for the first time, the *Histadrut*—the Israel labor movement—got a hearing from the United Hebrew Trades of New York. But by 1947, even before the establishment of the State of Israel, we are told that "the more immigrant Jewish workers become Americanized, the more enthusiastically they support the fund for Palestine and the Jewish State" (Joseph Schlossberg, "Foreword", *Cooperative Palestine,* by Kurland).

III

Judaism as a religious civilization has to reckon with the new forms in which this-worldly salvation is sought, out of the growing conviction that the place of human self-fulfillment is the earthly scene and not a heavenly hereafter. So long as salvation was conceived as other-worldly, the means of its attainment could easily be regarded as having been set forth in a fixed tradition that was as immutable as it was infallible. There was no way of testing the effectiveness of those means, since their consequences were regarded as taking place in a world which "neither eye hath seen nor ear hath heard." Religion was assumed to possess a validity that was independent of human experience and a significance that did not have to be stated in terms of human values. The voice of the past was far more authoritative than that of the present.

But when salvation becomes this-worldly, and manifests itself as the urge to raise human life to its .utmost perfection, the traditional means to achieve salvation find themselves subjected to the test of experience. The means to salvation must relate themselves to organic needs of human nature as well as to actual social, economic, cultural and political conditions. Human life, on any terms, is inconceiveable apart from a social group as its milieu and matrix; all the more so is salvation, or human life at its maximum. As the Talmud has it: "Give me society or give me death" (*Baba Batra,* 166b).

In the past, the society that was indispensable to salvation was based on actual or fictitious kinship and/or on some revelation vouchsafed to the founders of that society. If the former was the case, the society constituted a nation; if the latter, the society formed an ecclesia or church. In the past the Jews were a nation, in the ancient sense, and an ecclesia. That means they were both a historical community and a mystical body.

With the emergence of this-worldly salvation as the goal of human life, a new basis of unity for permanent societies has come into being: citizenship. The citizen, as distinguished from the subject, abides in a political relationship with his fellowmen, by virtue of a mutual agreement which, though tacit, is as valid as though it were expressed. The subject, if he is not a slave, is such by virtue of kinship, whether actual or fictitious, which is usually confirmed or sanctioned by some supernatural revelation. In backward societies, a person's status is determined primarily by some supernaturally revealed tradition which assigns to him a place in the universal order. "Just as in the West," we are told, "the first question when meeting a stranger concerns his nationality, in the East it is his religion ... 'There are no nations in Islam,' says an Arab proverb" (Raphael Patai, *Israel Between East and West,* pp. 39-40).

The concept of citizenship logically implies that the state, which represents the citizens of a modern nation, is the product of social contract. That does not mean that states as such are necessarily of a contractual character. It means only that whether a state, like the United States, came into existence recently, or, like Holland or England, evolved out of a pre-modern state, it must be considered as if its citizens had gone through the formality of a contractual arrangement. Such an arrangement implies that the modern state is based neither on race nor on creed, but on intrinsic and inalienable human rights of the individual citizen. Although, in practice very few states live up to this democratic conception of citizenship—and almost no state is entirely free from the influence of medieval or fundamentalist clericalism—the State of Israel will have to live up to it.

The conception of the state as the embodiment of a sovereignty inherent not in the members of a government but in the individual citizens could have arisen only in Holland and the Anglo-Saxon countries. There the free-church movement had prepared the way for the status of free citizenship. But the free-church movement went only half way toward the making of modern man. It continued to operate with other-worldly means of salvation. What a modern nation really needs, and what will undoubtedly come about in time, is a free-church movement which, in addition to stressing the inalienable dignity and status of the individual, will learn to foster the values essential to this-worldly salvation, such as justice, freedom and world brotherhood. "A state which is incompetent to satisfy different races condemns itself," wrote Lord Acton (*History of Freedom and Other Essays,* p. 297).

The most important, and at the same time most difficult problem to be solved is how to make social order and discipline compatible with freedom and voluntarism. Such compatibility is indispensable, if human nature is not to be defied, but served. To give voluntarism free rein is to invite nihilism. On the other hand, to suppress it, or even to fail to encourage it is to ignore the complexity and plurality that mark human nature. It should be the function of the democratic state to foster discipline, and

it should be the function of the religious body, whether church
or synagogue, to foster voluntarism. *That synthesis of discipline—
which calls for conformity—with voluntarism—which implies diversity—is the* novum *with which democracy is experimenting
in human society.* The attempt is new. For a long time to come
it is bound to be attended by considerable bungling. But unless
is succeeds, human society will fall back upon totalitarianism
as the only practicable social order. That will put an end to
individual freedom, the indispensable prerequisite to all that is
most worthy in human life.

The principle of voluntarism in religion, which in the United
States has led to the separation of church and state, was come
upon at first simply as a necessary *modus vivendi* to prevent the
transfer to the new world of the old world struggle among the
different churches for state power. Now, however, that the separation of church and state has become an integral part of American democracy, it is recognized as essential in order to keep
religion free from the corrupting influence of power politics and
enable it to "speak from outside society, free to praise and free
to rebuke ... It can build the inter-nation through representing
the supernational element in the heart of citizens."

Now that Israel is to be the homeland of the Jewish People
and its civilization, it will have to foster the kind of Jewish religion that can afford to be voluntaristic and that will renounce
all ambition to engage in power politics. Without having a voice
in the administration of the State of Israel, voluntaristic Jewish
religion, which is likely to be diverse in belief and practice, can
enhance the Jewish way of life in Israel and in the Diaspora.
For that reason *it is entirely within the province of the New
Zionism to make a special effort to work out ways and means
of instituting Jewish voluntaristic religion.*

IV

The whole picture of the contemporary revolution in the conception of the human person, the nation, the state, and the church
has as yet been but dimly grasped even by specialists. Those who
were active in the Zionist movement could not possibly have

been fully aware of all the problems involved in maintaining voluntarist religion in a democratic state, such as Jews would have to establish in Eretz Yisrael. Nor could they have been clearly oriented with regard to what would be needed in order to achieve a new basis of Jewish unity for those who were bound to remain in the Diaspora.

That, however, does not excuse Zionists today from the duty of facing the inescapable consequences of the idea of the democratic state, based on intrinsic and inalienable human rights of each citizen. In the light of those realities, *the State of Israel cannot be a Jewish State, nor can world Jewry continue to be a nation in the modern sense. The State of Israel will have to be an Israeli State, and world Jewry will have to be metamorphosed into a Jewish People which is rooted in Eretz Yisrael and which has its branches wherever it is allowed to live.*

It is amazing to note that Ben Gurion writing in *The New York Times Magazine* of March 28, 1954, speaks of "the re-emergence of the Jewish State," as though the State of Israel were the same kind of Jewish State as that which the Romans destroyed in the year 70. The failure to grasp the *novum* in the State of Israel is due to the confused notion that prevailed in the minds of Herzl and Nordau with regard to the type of state they envisaged. When Nordau married the Protestant widow of a deceased friend, and she was willing to embrace Judaism, Herzl advised against it. Herzl then wrote to him the following: "What are we today? Citizens of the ideal Jewish State, the establishment of which appears to us to be the most beautiful (engaging) content of our lives. When our work is done, I believe that a Jewish citizen, namely, a citizen of the Jewish State will not be forbidden to marry a foreigner. She will become politically Jewish, irrespective of her religion ... Incidentally, you could advance some striking precedents; if I am not mistaken, Moses was married to a Midianite" (*Max Nordau*, [French] by Anna and Max Nordau, pp. 98 f. cf. English translation).

Hobhouse points out how much more developed a modern nation is than one based on kinship, or than an ecclesia based on revelation (which he terms "authority"). "A modern nation," he says, "retains the element of mutuality and cooperativeness characteristic of the former, combines with it the extension of scale and regularity of order achieved by the authoritarian states, and adds a measure of freedom to the constituent parts and an elasticity to the whole, which are peculiarly its own" (cf. M. Ginsberg, *Idea of Progress*, p. 44).

That fact transforms the state from an end in itself to a means. Whereas in the old regime the individual existed for the state, now the state is conceived as existing for the individual. The main function of the state is so to organize the life of the nation that the individual shall be enabled not only to live, but to live well, and that he should come to look to the nation to redeem him from his own mortality. The State of Israel, however, will have to serve not only as a means to the well-being of the Israeli nation and all who constitute it, but also as a home for the Jewish People and its civilization. Thus, the State of Israel will fulfill in some respects a function analogous to that which the Italian State has been fulfilling in providing a home for the Roman Catholic Church. In other respects, however, the State of Israel will be as different from the Italian State as a democracy is different from a theocracy.

In general, the modern national state represents a transformation. Before the Protestant revolution, a national state was religiously homogeneous and subject to the Church. Now a state is a religiously heterogeneous and the trend of its political development must be toward regionalism. The State of Israel, therefore, can no more be a Jewish state than the United States can be an Anglo-Saxon state, although the dominant culture of the latter is Anglo-Saxon. Nor can it expect to be entirely independent and sovereign. "Nothing is more essential for the uninhibited growth of a people," writes Nahum Goldmann, "and most especially of the Jewish People, whose history demonstrates the permanence of ideas and the impermanence of states, than firm and unqualified repudiation of the barbaric and grotesque theory that the state is an end in itself . . . The time may come—and I hope it will come —when sovereign national states will be a memory of the past" ("Herzl and the Jewish State" in *Jewish Frontier*, Sept. 1954).

Nationalism is bound to give way sooner or later to super-national regionalism, governing the state's external relations. At present, there are two competing power groups, the Western and the Eastern, into whose orbits the minor states are being drawn.

What kind of society is present day Israel ? It certainly is not an ancient kind of nation, such as the Jews constituted in the past, since non-Jews are to have equality in every respect with Jews. Nor does it constitute the "Ecclesia of Israel," or religious nomocracy, which is what Rabbinism has made of World Jewry. What kind of society is World Jewry to be henceforth? It certainly cannot become a modern nation, since there is no political relationship between it and the State of Israel. *Upon the answers to these questions depends not only the relation of Diaspora Jewry to the Jews of Israel, but the fate of the historic Jewish People and the future of Judaism.*

Long before the establishment of the State of Israel, the group status of the Jews was an enigma. The answer given by the Paris Sanhedrin in 1806, and adopted by Classical Reform, has not been taken seriously, certainly not in Europe. Even in America, Kaufmann Kohler, the formost theologian of the Reform movement, maintained that "the *racial* community formed, and still forms, the basis of the religious community." In actual practice, neither "racial community" nor "religious community" has held Jews together.

"All Jews are united in fellowship only in relation to otherworldly matters," writes Joseph Hayyim Brenner ("Haarakhat Atzmenu" in *Kol Kitvei Y. H. Brenner,* Vol. VII, pp. 219-267), "but in relation to this-worldly matters they are alien to one another. Everyone is his own nearest relative. It appears that in the matter of self-love Jews are unique. We have no political capacity. That is to say, we are mere zeros."

"What then holds us together, since the dawn of Emancipation?" asks Franz Rosenzweig. "In what does the community of our contemporary life show itself, that community which alone can lead from the past to a living future? The answer is frightening. Since the beginning only one thing has unified the German Jews in a so-called Jewish life. Emancipation itself, the Jewish struggle for equal rights" (Quoted by Glatzer in *Franz Rosen-zweig*, p. 221). Similarily, the main unifying factor in American-Jewish life has been the struggle against anti-Semitism.

The Zionists who came near envisaging an all-embracing unity for the Jewish People, after the establishment of an independent State, were called "those who accept the *Galut*." But the nature of their acceptance is ambiguous. Do they conceive Diaspora as a normal and permanent condition, or merely as exile and therefore a temporary condition, and actually a necessary evil? The clearest statement on the subject is that formulated by Eliezer Rieger, who was one of the most influential educators in Israel, during the years immediately preceding and following its establishment. The following is what he had to say in 1939 on the subject of "the inter-dependence of Eretz Yisrael Judaism and the Judaism outside it."

"Anyone who has eyes in his head cannot help seeing that Eretz Yisrael cannot possibly absorb the myriads of Jews in *Galut* ... More powerful nations than we are—Germans, Poles, Italians, Irish, Greeks, etc.,—cannot absorb their nationals in their own countries, but try to strengthen them in whatever foreign countries they settle, by fostering their spirit, and at times even aiding them politically. Why then should we delude ourselves with impossible expectations and discourage the Hebrew *Gola* that wants to live? Why not 'bring forth the sweet from the strong' and the precious from that which is worthless? ... With the establishment of a Jewish State, the *Gola* might almost acquire 'normal status' ... That state of affairs obtained during the era of the Second Temple. The Jews outside Eretz Yisrael then exercised a great influence upon those within it. And equally great was the prestige of Eretz Yisrael among the Jews outside.

"Eretz Yisrael and the *Gola* are mutually indispensable. Without the *Gola* to encompass it, Eretz Yisrael will become parochial; and without Eretz Yisrael as its center the *Gola* is apt to deteriorate. The international character which Judaism possesses, and which at present is its curse, might serve—when the Hebrew land becomes a reality—as a powerful influence in the spiritual, the economic and the political aspects (of Jewish life).

"The revival of Hebrew culture can materialize fully only in Eretz Yisrael. In the countries outside it, the Jew is destined to be a hyphenated Jew, *i.e.*, a Polish-Jew, a German-Jew, an American-Jew. Jewish Jews, without any hyphen, can be only in Eretz Yisrael. *Only they can create a center for world Judaism* (italics mine) . . . The Jewish settlement in Eretz Yisrael will thus be the *avant garde* of the Jewish People and it will have to bear the responsibility for world Judaism" (*Hahinukh Haivri B'Eretz Yisrael,* pp. 247-248).

The foregoing is probably the clearest pronouncement that has come from those who, long before the establishment of the State, were sufficiently farsighted to reckon with the Jews who were bound to remain in the Diaspora. Unfortunately it made but little impression on Zionist thinking and on Jewish education in Israel. With all its clarity, however, it does not touch upon the kind of cultural or spiritual content which is to render Eretz Yisrael and Golah "mutually indispensable." Without a definite understanding as to what the nature of that content is to be, the "affirmation" of Diaspora Judaism is meaningless.

V

Pre-State Zionism was prevented by the urgency of the tasks at hand from thinking through the problem presented by the new kind of society Jews would have to form both in Israel and outside, if they were to survive as an identifiable Jewish collectivity. What exactly would be the relation of Jews to non-Jews in the prospective state in Eretz Yisrael and in the Diaspora was a question that was left entirely open. It never occurred to the Jews to expect Eretz Yisrael to be an *exclusively* Jewish country. They were content with the formula of 1922, which limited the immigration of Jews into Eretz Yisrael to the economic capacity of the country to absorb them. They were at all times willing to regard the nation that would arise in Eretz Yisrael as an amalgam of Jewish and Arab races.

Only now and then was a casual thought given to what might be the attitude of Jews in Eretz Yisrael to those in the Diaspora,

and it was generally one which foresaw complete severance with
the Jewish life there. Menaham Ussishkin told a teachers' convention in Jerusalem that, at a dinner in honor of writer Mendele
Mocher S'farim, he wished him to live to see the day when his
books would not be read any longer, because the Jews would come
to hate the *Galut* (state of exile) . . . "There is no reason why our
youth (in Eretz Yisrael)," continued Ussishkin, "should have
to study about life in the *Gola* (the lands of exile)" (Rieger,
Ibid., p. 242).

Pre-State Zionism could not have foreseen the great complexity of the problem of Jewish creative survival, whether in Israel or
in the Diaspora, arising from the trends toward humanism and
this-worldly ideas of salvation. That problem consists in the need
of acculturating Jews to Western civilization, without, at the same
time, abandoning the values by which Jews have lived as a People
during the past thirty-five centuries. That problem has to be solved,
otherwise Israel is likely to become a Levantine state with a mush-
room civilization, and Diaspora Jewry to be completely absorbed by
the majority populations.

A no less difficult task is to maintain among American Jews,
whose integration into Western culture goes on apace, sufficient
momentum of their tradition, and that sense of spiritual kinship
with the rest of Jewry which tradition has given them, to feel the
need of reconstituting themselves as a People and reclaiming Eretz
Yisrael as the spiritual homeland of Diaspora Jews.

A free nation like the United States makes it possible for Jews
not only to share in the high standard of living which it has attained, but also to strive for complete self-fulfillment in this world.
It is for Zionism so to define itself as to vindicate the right of those
American Jews who can make an important contribution to Israel,
by either settling there permanently, or for a time, to do so with
full conviction and condemned by none. No one finds fault with
the American-born poet Eliot for becoming an Englishman. He
felt that was the only way he could achieve his life goal.

Old-line Zionists find it hard to realize that American Jewry
represents an unprecedented phenomenon, as does America itself.
"Perhaps American Jewry does constitute an entirely new phe-

nomenon in Jewish history?" asks Livneh, "Perhaps it is not merely another *Galut*?" Yet even he, who should have known better, answers in the negative.

If Zionism is to redeem the Jewish People and regenerate its spirit, it has to broaden its own perspective, and undertake to cope with the two-fold problem of getting the traditionalists to accept the principle of separation of institutional religion from the state and reconstituting the Jewish People as an international People, with its nucleus in Israel.

The New Zionism should teach all Jews to regard their sense of unity and mutual responsibility both as a means and as a goal of their personal salvation, as that is understood in the modern mental climate. It should aim to foster, on the basis of our common history and tradition, a sense of interdependence and a process of interaction between the Jews of Israel and the Jews of the rest of the world. The societal organism that will evolve out of this interaction will be differently structured from the Jewish People of the past, but it will be morally and spiritually continuous with that People.

All this is in line with what Dr. Nahum Goldmann said in his keynote address at the First American Zionist Assembly, held in New York, on December 5, 1953:

"It may sound paradoxical, but it is true nevertheless, that Zionism will hereafter be judged by its efforts for Jewish survival outside of Israel maybe more than by its efforts on behalf of Israel ... No less than our obligation to see Israel through its difficult period is our obligation to defeat indifference, arrest assimilation, combat disintegration, for these dangers are more imminent today than in any previous period in our history."

"In consonance with this approach," we read in the *Jewish Frontier,* "the Assembly program and discussions were dominated by the theme that Zionism must come to grips with three major problems: 1) assuring the unity of the Jewish People, 2) educating our youth and Hebraizing Jewish life, and 3) relating the Jewish communities, and primarily Jewish youth, to the realities of Israel life, with a greater emphasis on *halutziut* as one of the essentials."

It is high time for Zionism to transcend the limited perspective of its first cultural and political gropings, and to become fully aware of itself as nothing less than a creative venture to transform the Jewish People into a new kind of society, a society which is dedicated to the quest for the Kingdom of God on earth, both in its own homeland and in cooperation with all other human societies. How is that to be achieved in the modern climate of opinion without severing the historic ties with the Jewish tradition? How shall we know what in that tradition is viable, and what does not lend itself to reinterpretation? These are questions which are as much a part of the Zionist movement as questions of an immediately practical nature. They may not be part of Zionist tactics, but they are part of that Zionist strategy without which all tactical gains are likely to be lost in a general defeat.

It is neither the task nor the responsibility of an individual to formulate the strategy of the Jewish future, including Zionism's part in that future. That is a task which only a responsible and duly authorized body of Jews eminent in various walks of life, and vitally interested in the perpetuation and development of the Jewish heritage, should undertake. They should formulate Jewish problems, suggest the solutions and determine the procedure for translating them into action.

This is not a matter for a single conference of an *ad hoc* assembly or conclave. Nothing less permanent than an established institution which functions as a center of learning and research, of inspiration and guidance can serve as an adequate instrument for the needed reconstruction of Jewish life both in Israel and in the Diaspora.

We may well learn in this instance from a section of civilization with which we Jews have thus far rarely been in contact. Buddhist civilization, too, is undergoing change, due to the challenge of the Western world. To meet that challenge, the Buddhist Great Council (see *Christian Century*, June 9, 1954) with the aid of the Burmese Government, is establishing at Rangoon a vast International Institute for Advanced Buddhistic Studies. The announcement concerning that Institute says that it "expects to serve all of southeast Asia, and be a means of strengthening the cultural and spiritual ties of that area and fostering and encouraging understanding between the East and the West."

Does it not seem most logical and fitting that a task similar to that of the Buddhistic Institute should be undertaken by the Hebrew University? Like that Institute, it should be international, and thus serve to strengthen the cultural and spiritual ties of Jews throughout the world. The Hebrew University is a creation of Diaspora Jews and still relies upon them for support. That support would be forthcoming in far greater measure, if the Hebrew University would assume the task of welding the Jewish People into a cultural and spiritual unity.

What follows is intended to serve merely as a starting point for the discussion of the New Zionism, as Pinsker's *Self-Emancipation,* or Herzl's *Jewish State,* served as a starting point in the discussion of what is generally known as political Zionism. Like those tracts, this one, too, seeks to motivate Jews to take action. The particular type of action to which this tract addresses itself consists of: 1) the reaffirmation of Jewish Peoplehood as a bond uniting all Jews throughout the world, 2) the normalization of Jewish life in the Diaspora, and 3) the fostering of a Jewish religious civilization to the extent local conditions in each country or region permit.

BIBLIOGRAPHY

SALO W. BARON, *Modern Nationalism and Religion*, N. Y., Harper and Bros., 1947.

MORRIS GINSBERG, *The Idea of Progress*, Boston, Beacon Press, 1951.

CARLTON J. H. HAYES, *Essays on Nationalism*, N. Y., Macmillan, 1926.

HORACE M. KALLEN, *Judaism at Bay*, N. Y., Bloch Publishing Co., 1932.

ARTHUR C. McGIFFERT, *The Rise of Modern Religious Ideas*, N. Y., Macmillan, 1919.

GEORGE FOOT MOORE, *The Birth and Growth of Religion*, N. Y., Scribners, 1930.

MILTON STEINBERG, *The Making of the Modern Jew*, Indianapolis, Bobbs-Merril, Co., 1934.

JUDD L. TELLER, *The Making of the Ideals that Rule Israel*, COMMENTARY, January, 1954.

——. *Labor Zionism Comes to Power*, COMMENTARY, February, 1954.

CHAPTER IV

The Reaffirmation of Jewish Peoplehood

APART FROM THE PRACTICAL PURPOSE of creating the political and economic conditions in Eretz Yisrael essential for Jews who wish to live there, pre-State Zionism, both cultural and political, has contributed toward a proper perspective on Jewish life, culture and religion by focusing attention on the Jewish People as the core, or main existential reality, which is central to all else that is Jewish. "A civilization," says the metaphysician R. S. Collingwood, "is a way in which people live, and if the way in which people live is an impracticable way, then there can be no question of saving it. What has to be saved is not the way of living but the people who live that way; and saving them means inducing them to live in a different way, a way that is not impracticable" (*Metaphysics* Oxford, 1940, p. 226).

From that standpoint, the vicissitudes of Judaism are the vicissitudes of the Jewish People in its effort to live and to help those who belong to it to achieve salvation, or to make the most of their lives. Hence, the emergence of Judaism from the crisis through which it is passing consists first and foremost in bringing the *Jewish People* out of its present perilous state of disintegration, and in setting up for it the specific goal of reintegration, or reconstitution.

What is involved in this procedure will become clear by realizing once again that the disintegration of Jewish solidarity began with the change in the conception of salvation. The most comprehensive political effect of the change in this conception from one centered on the hereafter to one centered on this world is the

rise of the modern order of society, which is based on citizenship
instead of on kinship or on revelation, on contract instead of on
status, and on consent instead of on authority.

Of all the movements in Jewish life only Reform has found
it necessary to cope with the problem arising out of this new type
of modern nationhood. For reasons to be noted later (Ch. V),
the solution proposed by Reform has proved unworkable. Even
Zionism, so far, has dealt with the problem in haphazard fashion,
leaving it at loose ends in Israel, and disclaiming the possibility
of solving it in the Diaspora. For the sake of the State of Israel,
however, insofar as it depends upon Diaspora Jewry, Zionism can
no longer afford to ignore the problem created by modern nationhood.

Avraham Harman of the Israel Consulate in New York, ad-
dressing a convention of Conservative rabbis, made some very
pertinent statements concerning the interdependence of the Jews
of Israel and those of the Diaspora. "The responsibility for the
continuity of Jewishness, however it may be conceived," he said,
"must be shared equally by all Jews wherever they are. . . . The
great danger in the 'center theory' of Judaism, is that the prophecy:
'The Law will come forth from Zion' may be interpreted to
mean that one section of the Jewish people will feel less responsibility for the continuity of Judaism than another section of the
Jewish people.

"The State of Israel came into existence only because of the
presence of Jewish responsibility outside Israel. The State of Israel
was the product of Jews outside Israel. Everything that is significant in Israel was not born in Israel. *Haganah* didn't start in
Israel; it started in Czarist Russia. Hebrew wasn't reborn in Israel,
it was reborn outside Israel as a modern language of literature
and speech and imported into Israel" (Avraham Harman, *Proceedings, The Rabbinical Assembly,* 1953, p. 269).

By the same token that Hebrew and *Haganah* had to be imported into Israel from European Zionism, the idea of the peoplehood of world Jewry and the indispensability of Jewish religion
may have to be imported from American Zionism.

I

The unity of world Jewry is the outgrowth of two interests which the Jew has to maintain for the sake of his this-worldly salvation. One is the development of the State of Israel as a modern democratic environment for Jewish civilization; the other is the oneness of the Jewish People, as bearer of a tradition which the Jew needs in order to validate his faith in the meaning of human life and the perfectibility of human nature.

"Group ties give a person support, security, and recognition, to say nothing of valuable bonds of friendship and trust. . . . The disintegration of the group tends to be followed by the breakdown of the moral conscience in the individual" (Karl Mannheim, *Diagnosis of Our Time*, pp. 106, 108). Hence Mannheim draws the conclusion that "democracies must do everything in their power to remedy the disintegrating effects of industrial civilization on our family and community life."

Insofar as the individual identifies himself with his People, whether it be church or nation, his personality comes to consist basically of the memories, experiences and hopes of that People. When, therefore, as in the case of many Jews, the individual finds that his Jewishness stands in the way of his aspirations, and he comes to hate his People, he cannot help at the same time hating that in his own personality which is Jewish, whether biologically or socially inherited. That is the common variety of self-hate to which many Jews nowadays are subject. But so long as that self-hate gives rise only to a neurotic condition and has not yet attained the psychotic condition of insanity, the Jew who suffers from it, unhappy as he is, cannot normally wish he were changed into a non-Jew. No normally-minded person would wish to become happy by losing his identity and taking an altogether different character.

"The group to which an individual belongs is the ground on which he stands . . ." writes Kurt Lewin. "The firmness or weakness of this group might not be consciously perceived just as the firmness of the physical ground on which we tread is not always thought of. Dynamically, however, the firmness and clearness of this ground determine what the individual wishes to do, what he

can do, and how he will do it. This is true equally of the social
ground as of the physical" (*Resolving Social Conflicts*, p. 174).

We cannot agree with Lewin, however, when he says that
the problem of belongingness which confronts the Jewish person
can be solved, if he comes to understand that "whether the Jewish
group is a racial, religious, national or cultural one, the fact that
it is classified by the majority as a distinct group is what counts."
He calls that fact "the *interdependence of fate* with the rest of
American Jews and indeed with Jews all over the world" (*Ib.*, p.
184). That interpedendence of fate may merely create a permanent
state of neurosis. *There is no reason why that interdependence of
fate may not be converted into an interdependence of will by a
formal commitment.*

The first time in modern times the Jews needed to reaffirm
their Jewish solidarity came with the organization of the *Alliance
Israelite Universelle* in 1860. When the Jews of Western Europe,
who had been granted civil rights, realized that they might forfeit
those rights in the wake of the anti-Semitic outbreak against Jews
in Damascus in 1840, an awareness of interdependence of fate
between themselves and Jews in the remotest part of the world at
last dawned upon them. That is evident in the first appeal issued
by the *Alliance,* which read somewhat as follows: "If you who are
scattered into all corners of the globe and who are dispersed among
the nations possess any sense of unity in your hearts and in your
will, however slight, through the ancient faith; if you are certain
that this unity is a source of blessing; . . . if all this is self-evident
to you, Jews of the world respond to our call and help us."

Unfortunately, there was no other purpose envisaged by the
Alliance than that of improving the material lot of Jews as individuals. There was no collective ideal like the enhancement of
Jewish religion, or the creativity of Jewish life, contemplated in
any of its activities. The main purpose was to westernize the Jews,
not only of the European continent but also of the Near East and
of North Africa, generally as part of the larger, though not stressed,
plan to facilitate their absorption by the rest of the world. In time,
the Jews of England, Germany and Austria broke away from the
Alliance and established similar organizations of their own, which

were often used by their respective governments to advance their own colonial plans.

II

If proof were needed that the survival of Judaism fundamentally depends on the survival of the Jewish People, we would have only to point to what has been happening to the Jewries of those countries in which their only distinctive bond of unity has been Jewish religion. In France, England, Germany, Holland, the Scandinavian countries, the Jews have been gradually disappearing. How ineffective religion alone is in keeping itself alive is shown by the fact that even the moral and financial encouragement of government is unable to sustain it. For those very countries, in which Judaism has been deteriorating and Jews are being gradually absorbed, extended government support to the religious institutions with which Jews were expected to affiliate themselves.

Zionism now has to find a new collective category for Jews throughout the world which would constitute them as a new society. Before the establishment of the State of Israel the Jews fitted into the category of "nationality" as applied by Carlton J. H. Hayes (*Essays on Nationalism,* p. 51) to "a group of people who speak either the same language or closely related dialect, who cherish common historical traditions, and who constitute or think they constitute a distinct cultural society." For us Jews, the continued use of Hebrew and a life of Torah met the foregoing requirements.

Nationalism means "an actual historical process, that of establishing nationalities as political units, of building out of tribes and empires the modern institution of the national state" (*Ibid.*). From that standpoint, pre-State Zionism was an expression of Jewish nationalism. For reasons stated in the previous chapters, however, Zionism can no longer continue in this role. It has to evolve into a New Zionism, the purpose of which would be to reorganize the social structure of Jews throughout the world and spur them to cooperate for their moral and spiritual regeneration. Not nationhood, but peoplehood, would be the objective of the New Zionism, since it would have to embrace the entire House, or Community, of Israel.

World Jewry will have to constitute an international People, with the Jewish community in the State of Israel as its nucleus. The term "People" is used here merely in anticipation of the particular category that a conference is likely to agree on as the appropriate one for the Jewish coroporate entity to assume. By the same token we can only surmise what form it will take on. Superficially it will resemble a spiritual organism like an ecclesia, as embodied in the Synagogue or in the Church. But it will differ from them in the way it will function. In the *first* place, it will not be based upon a revealed edict, but upon the desire of all who belong to it to achieve salvation, or maximum self-fufillment, as human beings. *Secondly,* it will resemble the Synagogue, but not the Church, in three respects: 1) it will be rooted in a localized history and tradition—namely, that of Eretz Yisrael; 2) it will continue to be nourished by a localized community, the Jewish community of Eretz Yisrael; 3) it will be regulated in accordance with a code, conformity to which will be solely on the basis of voluntary commitment.

The foregoing suggestions are only intended to illustrate concretely wherein the category "People" would differ from any of the existing types of social organisms.

The fact that a People would be a new kind of social organism is no reason for ruling it out as impracticable. The progress of civilization has been made possible through the rise of new societal groupings and structures to serve as means of satisfying newly acquired human needs. The Jews as a corporate entity have passed through organic metamorphoses, from a federation of tribes to an integral nation, and from an integral nation to an ecclesia.

Each such metamorphosis marks a new stage in the evolution of mankind. Our ancestors attained nationhood when they federated their tribes through a covenant with YHWH who became their national God. They were the first to achieve a social maturity which the other groups were long in attaining. Those got as far as tribalism and city-statehood. Even when they did attain political unity on a large scale, as in the case of the Roman Empire, they really never got beyond city-statehood. The City of Rome remained to the end the axis around which the whole empire revolved.

Even making divinities out of the emperors, and imposing emperor worship throughout the length and breadth of the empire, failed to bring about a deep sense of unity among its far flung populations.

On the other hand, our ancestors early aspired to national unity which they expressed in the only way they knew—namely, by concluding a covenant with the God YHWH, whom they credited with their escape from Egypt and their success in taking possession of the land which became the seat of their civilization. The sense of national unity took a long time to penetrate the minds and hearts of our ancestors. After overcoming the tendency to pay homage to other gods, and to merge with the peoples of those gods, they had to cope with the fragmentation of their nationhood in the worship of YHWH at many local sanctuaries. But this practice, too, was finally eliminated when the worship of YHWH became centralized in the one Temple at Jerusalem. That is without parallel in the history of other peoples, as is the strong sense of nationhood which resulted from that centralization of worship.

Our ancestors matured socially still further when, from being a nation based on blood kinship, they thought of themselves as an ecclesia, ready to admit proselytes. The Prophets who emphasized the ethical aspect of the religion of YHWH contributed to the universalization of his Godhood. That idea finally took root in the Jewish consciousness only after the dream of Alexander the Great to Hellenize the world had begun to materialize. Western mankind took over from the Jews the concept of ecclesia when Rome become Christian. It then skipped nationhood by letting the City of Rome retain its hegemony over the Roman Empire. The other-worldliness of Christianity made that leap necessary.

With the Renaissance and the rise of this-worldliness, Western mankind began to mature into nationhood. When we trace the development of the nationalist movement in the Western world, we note that it first came to the fore in England with the advent of Puritanism. "The English Revolution," writes Hans Kohn, "was a synthesis of far-reaching importance of Calvinist ethics and a new optimistic humanism. Being a Calvinist Revolution, the new nationalism expressed itself in an identification of the English people with the Israel of the Old Testament" (*The Idea of Nationalism*, pp. 166, 174, and note p. 632).

By now, nationalism has become a dynamic religion which is taken seriously. Whether it is a good or an evil depends upon its objective. Historically it was a good, when it was directed against the arbitrary will of the medieval Church, or against the secular power wielded by kings or nobles. It becomes an evil, when it is directed against individual freedom. This ambivalence which nationhood manifests is common to any and all expressions of human nature, whether in the individual or in the group. To discourage or suppress nationhood because of the abuses to which it is liable is as unwarranted as to declare any natural or normal desire illegitimate because it is very often misdirected. The need of belonging to a history-making and potentially immortal group is inherent in the human being, as soon as he achieves a certain degree of social maturity. To thwart it is to interfere with the exercise of an inalienable human right.

The situation in which we Jews find ourselves should impel us to realize the dangers inherent in the contemporary religion of nationalism, and to take the next step toward social maturity by developing a form of corporate unity which preserves the intrinsic values of nationhood while preventing its wrong uses. That corporate unity would not be based either on kinship, revelation or citizenship, but on the striving for salvation or maximum self-fulfillment as human beings, in the deepest and most inclusive sense.

III

As there were specific motivations for each new stage in the social maturation of the Jewish People, so there is need for identifying the motive underlying the reconstitution of Jews from a religious nation in exile into a permanent international and religious People. That motive will have to be religion, in the sense of some salvational ideal in terms of both individual and universal good.

The suggestion that Jews be reconstituted into a society with a common bond of religion has to be understood in the context of a this-worldly conception of religion. That kind of religion is possible only when the group it seeks to unite has a common background of history that was enacted in a particular land, and of a destiny in which that land continues to play an important role.

Moreover, in making religion the chief unifying factor, Jews would not be merely reverting to a primitive manifestation of nationhood. Religion would be chosen as this factor after weighing various alternatives. First of these would be blood kinship, as the term *nation* implies. Greek, Roman and Teutonic mythologies bear testimony to that fact. The exigencies of life, as they happened to obtain in 19th century Germany, where different races lived within common borders and spoke a common language, made it urgent for them to find some this-worldly bond of unity other than blood kinship. That need led the outstanding German thinkers to select common language as the chief nation-making instrument (*Cf.* W. A. Dunning, *A History of Political Ideas,* pp. 299, 312, 325). Later geography was stressed as the nation-making factor.

The question of the decisive nation-making factor—whether kinship, language, or territory—arose during the political struggle for national independence and sovereignty. It might again arise with regard to the State of Israel and the Israeli nation now in the making. In all likelihood, territory will there be the chief nation-making factor. But nothing of this applies to the collective organism to be known as the Jewish People.

The problem presented by world Jewry is undoubtedly unique. Jews no longer wish to accept common ancestry, or kinship, as the main unifying element. That is too reminiscent of Nazism. Language by itself is meaningless as a unifying element, unless it arises out of shared day-to-day interests. That can be the case only in Israel. But for Jewry as a whole only a common religion based on a long tradition like that of the Jewish People, and which can be made to include language, culture and day-to-day human interests growing out of involvement in the nuclear segment of the

Jewish community in Israel, can and should serve as a uniting bond.

Judaism will have to be conceived as a *non-creedal* religious civilization, centered in loyalty to the body of the Jewish People throughout the world. Its religious articulation should take place through autonomous institutions of learning, congregations and societies, and hypothetical rather than authoritative theologies. All Jewish group activities should be conducted in conscious dedication to the solidarity of the Jewish People and the growth of its ethical and spiritual consciousness. If Jews are to have a mission, a purpose serving as criterion and measure of its endeavors, they can choose none more worthy than that of demonstrating the humanizing influence of a religion that encourages freedom of thought and unity in the diversity of democratic social structure.

IV

It is a fact that Zionist spokesmen have always dealt gingerly, if at all, with religion in relation to Jewish nationhood. There is more than one reason for that. In the first place, they were afraid that they might become involved in bitter controversy. Secondly, neither those who viewed religion as dispensable, as did Ahad Ha'am, or as indispensable, as does Buber, have dealt with it as a natural phenomenon, or as a manifestation of human nature, in the individual and in the group. To Ahad Ha'am and to Buber, as to European thinkers generally, humanist or liberal religion is a contradiction in terms. Their quarrel with those who treat religion dynamically is not merely one of semantics. It is a quarrel as to what is *authentic* religion.

Had they accepted the authenticity of dynamic religion, they would have realized that religion, as a form of human behavior, includes three radically different types of phenomena:

In the first place, religion is a term usually given to all human practices aimed at obtaining from some extra-human or super-human source the power needed to ward off harm and to satisfy the desires. A more accurate term for that type of religion is "magic."

A second type of religion is piety. It is the pattern of conduct based upon the emotions of loyalty, reverence and gratitude for the source of one's being. Though always directed toward God, the underlying *motif* is attachment to one's land, to one's people, or to both.

A third type of religion emphasizes ethics, or those traits and human relationships which enable human beings to live in a spirit of justice, peace and mutual helpfulness.

To which of these types a person's religion belongs depends upon his intellectual development, his emotional maturity and his ethical character. These three aspects of his personality determine what he regards as his salvation or self-fulfillment.

The trouble with those who are indifferent, or antagonistic, to religion is that they identify it with the first type, which is essentially magic. Magic as a means of acquiring power to ward off harm and to obtain one's desires has been replaced by science and technics. They, therefore, conclude that religion has become an anachronism. They forget that we cannot do without loyalty to, gratitude and reverence for the sources of our being, or without submitting whatever power we possess to the control of ethical principles, sanctioned by a sense of their transcendent rightness.

That was the misunderstanding under which the majority of the *Maskilim* labored, a misunderstanding that must now be corrected. The only way to correct it is to take seriously the fact that religion is not a static system of belief and practice, but a dynamic response to man's need to give meaning to his life, or to experience the feeling that, if we will it, salvation or self-fulfillment may well be our lot. It is, therefore, not only possible but necessary to eliminate from the Jewish religion whatever survivals of magical practice or belief still exist in it, and to cultivate the religion of piety and ethics.

Jewish religion will then come to mean *that* in the Jewish tradition which is an expression of man's concern for his salvation or self-fulfillment.

V

Whatever idea man has of God is a correlate, or reflection, of that which he regards as salvation, or the fulfillment of human destiny. In religion, other than magic, God always signifies the Power that makes for salvation. The metaphysical conception of God, which depends upon one's idea of ultimate reality, is not, or should not be the subject matter of religion. The God of religion is, essentially, the God of a society, whether clan, tribe, nation, church, or people to which one belongs, and whose way of life is accepted as indispensable to salvation. To the Jew, therefore, God is the God of the Jewish People, insofar as it is to him a medium of salvation. If he is a traditionalist, he believes that its way of life was revealed by God. If he is a modernist, he regards its way of life as revealing God. That this is the meaning of God in human experience is implied in Franz Rosenzweig's statement: "It is only by jointly calling upon Him that we become a 'We' " (*Understanding the Sick and the Healthy*, p. 79).

What is meant by a People's being an instrument of salvation can perhaps be made clear by what is implied in the fact that, for the individual human being, his own personality is both the instrument and object of salvation. The implication is that, in order to achieve salvation, the individual must experience a sense of unbroken continuity which runs through all the changes in his own life. He cannot be a responsible person, unless he acts on the assumption that he is committed to contracts he made in the past, and the fulfillment of which is to take place in the future.

By the same token, that part of our personality which is identified with the People to which we belong demands, for its salvation, that the People be viewed as a corporate entity which continues as an identical being or process throughout all its vicissitudes. We share its corporate commitments and aspirations. To the extent that this sharing contributes to our moral and spiritual growth, it constitutes religious experience. *This self-identification of the individual Jew with his Jewish People is the source of the mystical element in the Jewish religion.* Why that is so becomes evident when we stop to consider what it is we characterize as mystical in any experience that we undergo.

In the first place, we characterize as mystical anything which we regard as indispensable to our life as human persons, without being able to explain why that is so, on logical or rational grounds. We accept our parents and our community with all their ways as the indispensable foundation of our lives. Why that is so is a mystery. Secondly, whatever experience gives us a feeling of direct personal contact or *rapport* with what we consider to be ultimate Reality we refer to as mystical. If we have a perceptive eye for the beauties of nature, any landscape, or seascape, or starry night meets that requirement, and therefore puts us in a mystical frame of mind. The same is true, if we have an ear for music. Not only the works of the great musical masters, but even a simple melody that sings from the heart, evokes a mystic response.

What the Jewish People should mean to the individual Jew may be illustrated by the famous answer given by George Malory, one of the greatest mountain climbers, when asked why he wanted to climb Everest. He simply replied: "Because it is there." Likewise when we are asked: "Why remain Jews?", the only reason we should feel called upon to give is: "Because the Jewish People is here and we are part of it." Unless we feel that to belong to the Jewish People is a high spiritual adventure which has intrinsic value regardless of consequences and practical ends, our Jewishness is tantamount to the interest of casual tourists in foreign countries.

Since the Jewish People is indispensable to the Jew as a human person, and since it has always given him the feeling of being in *rapport* with God, identification with the Jewish People provides Jewish religion with the indispensable dimension of the mystical. On the face of it, nothing should seem more obvious, yet it is the very obviousness that seems to have led many a Jewish thinker and theologian to develop a blind spot for the mystic character of this self-identification with the Jewish People. They seem to see in it only the socio-psychological significance which the non-Jewish social scientist, as an outsider, can see in it. But if they would stop to consider for one moment the entire regimen of Jewish religious practice and ritual, and note the extraordinary fact that the individual Jew never takes part in them

without associating himself with the whole House of Israel, they
would begin to sense the extent to which this association with the
Jewish People is not merely a socio-psychological, but a definitely
mystical, experience.

VI

The reason both Jewish and Gentile interpreters of Jewish
religion have failed to comprehend what is at the heart of its
mystery—and a religion must have a mystery at its vital center,
or it is lifeless—is that they have, almost to a man, regarded it
as ritual-centered. That misunderstanding may be said to have
arisen with the Apostle Paul, who identified religion with the Law,
and identified the Law mainly with ritual practice.

Another reason, no doubt, for failing to appreciate the mystical significance of Jewish Peoplehood as the core of Jewish religion
is that both Jewish and Gentile interpreters of it have assumed
that attaching such significance to Jewish Peoplehood would place
Jewish religion on the same level with the ancient ethnic religions,
which have, assumedly, been displaced by monotheism. Were Jewish religion anything less than pure monotheism, it would scarcely
be worthy of a place alongside the two world religions of Christianity and Islam.

All such reasoning is based upon unreflective assumptions
concerning religion. It would take us entirely too far afield to
point out what is wrong with those assumptions. But the one
basic fallacy underlying them is the assumption that Christianity
and Islam do *not* have as their core the same mystical factor of
a dedicated community as does the Jewish religion. The fact,
however, is that Christianity possesses that mystical factor in its
doctrine of the Mother Church, and Islam possesses it in the
"Community of Believers." The Jewish religion differs from those
two world religions in being satisfied to discover divinity in the
history and experiences of the People that evolved it, whereas they
prefer to look for the manifestation of divinity in their mission to
conquer the entire world.

In view, however, of the common misunderstanding that prevails concerning the true significance of the ethnocentricity of

Jewish religion, it is difficult to reconcile Jewish religion with an internationally dispersed Jewish People as a permanent condition of its existence. For that reason it will require considerable effort by an authorized Jewish assembly to master the complexities of Jewish peoplehood. Only after such effort will they be in a position to come before the world with a definition of the status of the Jewish People and a spelling out of the validity of its religion from the standpoint of a democratic social order in which the freedom and dignity of the human person are axiomatic.

Since human life is anything but static, any idea of salvation, or of God, must be dynamic. Since, in every stage of human development, man seeks to achieve his maximum potential, he inevitably treats the societal group whose experience he shares as the instrument of his salvation. As such an instrument, the societal group mediates for him the reality of God. That explains why belonging to a People or Church which bases its unity upon the common aspiration of its adherents to be "saved" expresses more than just a political need. It is an expression of a psychological need in which the entire person is involved. Unless, therefore, there is some concrete means of identifying that People or Church, the need for belonging is frustrated. No ghost people or invisible church can answer that need. This is illustrated by the following statement by Horace L. Friess, one of the outstanding leaders of the Ethical Culture movement. Referring to the fact that there is "within the Ethical movement this present wanting of a clearer and stronger unity," he adds: "Others say that we now need identifying symbols and moving forms of shared expression. Genuine symbols, of course, are not to be had for the asking. And when teachers in our Sunday Schools ask how the children are to identify their 'belonging,' their question has proved a poser to us" ("A Unity of Spirit," in *The Standard*, May-June, 1954).

Consequently, the motivation for Jewish unity should be the wish to make the Jewish People (with which we are identified through the fact of our being born into it as well as through the idea of us in the minds of the rest of the world) a fit instrument of this-worldly salvation, with all that that implies. The main implication is that we have to concentrate upon so improving the political, economic and other social conditions within the orbit of our influence as to make of this world a Kingdom of God. The entire tradition of the Jewish People should make it capable of counteracting the sinister by-products of this-worldliness, which are falsely ascribed to the modern regard for reason and experience as criteria of truth. Those by-products derive from the tendency to reduce all values to physical or mechanical facts and relationships and to reduce man to an object of calculation and control bereft of all ethical responsibility and spiritual worth.

It is just as mistaken to treat all self-identification with a People as "phenomenologically speaking the definition of a political act," as it would be to treat self-identification with a Church as a political act. What kind of an act self-identification with a People is depends upon the purpose for which we identify ourselves with it, whether it be political, economic, cultural or religious.

Judaism as a dynamic religious civilization is a synthesis of peoplehood, culture, and religion. In this entire discussion, peoplehood is assumed to be primary in the same sense that life is primary as compared with any of its products. The practical significance of this approach to Judaism becomes apparent, when we wish to get at the basic motive for giving children a Jewish education. "Education does not mould man in the abstract," says Karl Mannheim, "but in and for a given society, and the ultimate educational unit is never the individual but the group, which may vary in size, aim and function" (*Diagnosis of Our Time*, p. 81).

Of utmost significance is the fact that if the Jews were to reconstitute themselves into a religious People, they would demonstrate the validity of the principle concerning religion as an instrument of this-worldly salvation. That principle means that to be such an instrument, religion has to be indigenous or native to a particular land, whose everyday concerns give rise to the belief in God. The universal values which religion furnishes do not exist as abstract principles, but are expressed in the way the problems are solved and the interests satisfied, by virtue of their being related to the belief in God. The Jewish religion has always retained its indigenous character. On the other hand, the great world religions have been for the most part, derived or grafted.

Besides the advantage of being indigenous, the Jewish religion has the additional advantage of being capable of serving as an instrument of this-worldly salvation, without breaking with its own tradition. That is possible, because the *foundation* of Jewish religion, which is laid in the Jewish Scriptures, is free from such other-worldly notions of salvation as became an integral part of post-biblical religion. Thus, in addition to the intrinsic value of attaching the Jewish People to its past, which the cultivation of Bible-mindedness is certain to achieve, it is also needed to redirect our moral and spiritual interest to matters of this-worldly concern. As far as the Rabbinic stage of Judaism is concerned, its permanent values are such that they cannot be ignored, despite its other-worldly orientation.

VII

Jewish peoplehood is no longer possible without a Jewish community in Eretz Yisrael, as the majority population, to determine the character of the civilization there. *Hence the consolidation of the State of Israel should be based on the desire to provide the setting in which the Jewish People could become a fit instrument of this-worldly salvation for every Jew, wherever he resides.*

The effort to reconstitute ourselves as an international People is validated from the standpoint of natural rights on the following grounds:

a. The persistence in the Gentile consciousness of Jews as an identifiable group.

b. The inalienable right to existence of any group that does not interfere with the freedom of any other group.

c. The inalienable right of the individual to belong to whatever group he deems essential to his salvation, provided it does not interfere with any other, in the matter of salvation.

The individual Jew who regards this world as the scene of salvation depends upon the Jewish People to help him achieve it. For that reason, he must be able to feel that in investing the best part of himself in the Jewish People, he is investing in something that has a worthwhile future, and thereby achieving an earthly immortality.

Earthly immortality has become a basic need, in view of the obsolescence of the belief in supermundane immortality. The general state of mind with regard to other-worldly immortality is perhaps best expressed in Dilthey's diary, which speaks of another life as something which it would be cheap to deny, but confusing to take seriously (Horace L. Friess, "William Dilthey," *Journal of Philosophy*, June 3, 1929).

Personal immortality can be taken seriously, without confusing the mind, if we learn to view personality as that function of the human body which reveals God as the Power that makes for man's salvation. To the extent that we achieve such personality, we achieve immortality. There is objective truth, as well as poetry, in the following lines by Wordsworth in "To Toussaint L'Ouverture":

"Thou has left behind
Powers that will work for thee; air, earth and skies,
There's not a breathing of the common wind
That will forget thee; thou hast great allies;
Thy friends are exultations, agonies,
And love, and man's unconquerable mind."

To fail to take immortality seriously is bound to lead to the moral disintegration of human life. Man is aware of his ultimate personal decline and death and of the precariousness of life, even if he tries to forget them. That awareness is liable to lead to a regimen of living expressed in the verse: "Let us eat and drink for tomorrow we die." The life force that impels man to live also impels him to generate. It also impels him to live in a way that makes life possible not only for his children but also for the generations to follow them. That has given rise to the belief in a hereafter.

The hereafter, conceived as supermundane, plays a diminishing role in man's consciousness. On the other hand, responsibility for the influence of our conduct on the environment, and on what is likely to eventuate in the hereafter on this earth, cannot be ignored without making our own lives meaningless and decreasing the chances of human survival.

According to Paul Tillich, religion and philosophy, as far as they maintain the idea of "eternal life" as present in the temporal and transitory existence, do so by affirming that "the happiness which cannot be drawn from the present reality must and can be drawn from the anticipation of a future reality." He credits the idealistic socialistic movements of the nineteenth and twentieth centuries with having provided "happiness by anticipation" for those who struggle for "a new order of life" (*Cf.* "Freedom in the Period of Transformation" in *Freedom,* ed. Ruth Nanda Anshen, p. 143).

VIII

If we are to envisage the Jewish People of the future as an international group or fellowship, like the Church, we must expect it to assume different forms of communal structure and ideological validity in accordance with the different political conditions that obtain in the countries where Jews live. Our main concern at this point, however, is American Jewry and the ideological validity of its communal structure.

That the United States is a free nation, and that its nationalism is not of the exclusive type, is the result both of fortunate historical circumstances and of ethical purpose. No cultural religious community or denomination in the United States can cherish the hope of becoming the majority of the American nation. It is also true, however, that the overwhelming majority of the American nation identifies as Christian its religious feeling for life. Chief Justice Earl Warren spoke of the United States as "a Christian land governed by Christian principles," and as "a beacon light of faith for all the world" (*The New York Times,* February 5, 1954).

Though the Roman Catholic group is the largest minority in the United States, it can never become the majority population. It constitutes a segregated cultural entity. It insists upon developing its own exclusiveness as a religious culture to a far greater degree than Jews are in a position to do. "The Roman Catholic Church, like the Protestant churches, finds its chief springs of wealth and power in the United States" (Allen Nevins, "Should American History be Rewritten?", *The Saturday Review,* February 6, 1954).

What is legitimate to the Roman Catholic group in a free nation like the United States is equally legitimate to any other cultural or civilizational group, particularly if that group serves as an indispensable source of salvation to its members. The New Zionism, in urging the Jews of the Diaspora to adopt the principle of living in two civilizations, is not proposing that Jews should ask for themselves a privilege which their Gentile fellow-citizens are not enjoying. On the contrary, the principle of living in two civilizations is of the very essence of modern democratic national-ism, which makes room for the Church to maintain its historic life and civilization.

That applies perhaps with less force to the Protestant than to the Catholic Church, since Protestantism has, on the whole, allowed modern nationalism to pre-empt many of its cultural and social functions. Nevertheless, there is enough in common among all Protestant groups throughout the world to give their members a sense of having a stake in the same religious civilization. "The Church," wrote W. B. Brown, "is a universal society. Divided though it may outwardly be into independent communions with differing history and traditions, *the members are conscious of a common loyalty which makes the fortunes of their fellow Christians in other countries a matter of concern to them. American Chris-tians cannot be indifferent to what Christians in Germany or in Russia are experiencing"* (italics mine) (*Church and State,* 1936, p. 21). Note the reference to a common loyalty to a transnational group as in no way being in conflict with loyalty to the American nation.

It would not be difficult to make out a case against the claim of the Christian Church, whether Catholic of Protestant, to status not merely coordinate with that of the nation, but of primacy and superiority (*Cf. Free Churches and Christian Unity,* by Marion John Bradshaw). The Church teaches that "all power is of God, who made heaven and earth," that "all power in heaven and earth has been given to Christ," and that "all churches alike are obligated, in true ecumenical manner, to claim for Christ the whole world and all aspects of life." Taken literally, these teachings imply that the clergy and those to whom they delegate authority have a valid claim to make such use of the "power of God" as they deem proper. Any social order that submits to this kind of doctrine is bound to be monolithic.

It is likewise true that modern nationalism, with its rejection of the concept of power as deriving from the consent of the governed, and with all the consequences that flow from it, might also lead, as it has actually led in the case of Communism, Fascism and Nazism, to a monolithic social order. Fortunately, the democratic insistence on the inalienable rights of the individual to "life, liberty and the pursuit of happiness" has achieved a *modus vivendi* whereby the claims of Church and nation have been modified. That has made it possible for Church and nation to serve each other, and to be essential to each other, by toning down their respective arrogance and aggressiveness and in mutually providing what the other lacks. The nation provides the substance of human life, the Church, the goals. Given this *modus vivendi*, living in two civilizations has become an inescapable necessity, particularly when one civilization is religious and the other secular. The religious civilization needs down-to-earth tasks to prove its ability to better men's characters. The secular civilization needs that larger vision which is essential to world peace and international good will.

Religious minorities should, therefore, be viewed not only as legitimate, but as necessary. They have to fulfill the important function of preserving personal liberty. "The chief enemy of liberty is nationalism, the very thing which liberty itself created when it rescued nations from feudal tyranny, or the overlordship of kings" (James T. Shotwell, "Freedom, Its History and Meaning," in *Freedom,* ed. Anshen, p. 13).

What prevents nationalism from being benign and transforms it into a malignant force is mainly the constant threat of war. "There is every reason to wish," wrote Franz Boas, "that the cultural diversity of different groups, generally national groups, should be encouraged, and each be given the fullest opportunity to develop along its own line, but this has nothing to do with modern nationalism which is based on the assumption, often too true, that every nation is the enemy of all others, and therefore in duty bound to protect its members and itself. Thus nationalism becomes concentrated upon the idea of developing power, not national culture, power to defend itself, power to attain national unity, power to break its dangerous neighbors. The cultural mission of nationalism is lost sight of in the desire to be free of the power of aggression" (*This I Believe* I, ed. Raymond Swing, p. 26).

The religious minorities should help to preserve individual freedom by exercising "the constant, if conservative, criticism of the institutions, as well as habits which we have inherited from the past" (*Ibid.*, p. 20). From the standpoint of that function, every religion, or religious civilization, is in a position to communicate to its adherents the consciousness of "spiritual exile." The ancient Rabbinic equivalent for "spiritual exile" was the conception of the *Shekhinah* as being in exile. The homeless existence of the Jewish People was regarded by the Jews as an eclipse of God's power. It was, therefore, equated with the exile of His *Shekhinah*. Now that the homelessness of the Jewish People is to be ended, Jewish religion should interpret "the exile of the *Shekhinah*" in a broad sense, as synonymous with the universally disordered, disoriented and alienated condition of human life, and make the correction of that condition its dominant purpose.

IX

American Jews will have to translate their religious peoplehood into the institutional and cultural forms of their own American milieu. This can happen only if those who head the various Jewish organizations, whether in a lay or in a professional capacity, are thoroughly imbued with the desire to revitalize Jewish life and make it a source of salvation for the individual Jew.

At present we have Jewish self-segregation which is the product of unconscious social forces. It is sterile of any meaningful values. Jews are organized into fraternal orders, federations and welfare funds, public relations organizations, and social clubs. They tend to concentrate in particular neighborhoods. When they move away from those neighborhoods, they are soon followed by those from whom they flee. Jews even join congregations mainly for social rather than for religious reasons. Jewish education is at present devoid of any clear idea of the nature or status of Jews as a corporate entity, integration into which should be, in theory as well as in practice, the main purpose of that education.

Each institution, organization and financial drive is viewed as an end in itself, unrelated to any over-all pattern of Jewish life which should normally animate all of them. On the other hand, organic community would require their being related integrally to the Jewish People and its future. It is that spirit which the New Zionism has to infuse into the communal life of Diaspora Jewry. That is entirely different from the purpose for which Zionists in Eastern Europe, before and after the first World War, engaged in *Gegenwartsarbeit,* when they tried to capture the communities and convert them into instruments of the Zionist movement.

An organic Community should function as follows: It should (1) maintain a complete register of vital statistics and establish bureaus for gathering information concerning all matters of importance to Jewish life; (2) induce every Jew to affiliate with some local or national Jewish organization for the perpetuation of Jewish life; (3) budget all the needs of Jewish life, so as to give the individual Jew an idea of how he is to budget his own contributions to Jewish life; (4) activate the high ethical standards transmitted in the Jewish tradition, by the formation of specific codes and sanctions for various social and economic relationships; (5) foster and coordinate Jewish educational, cultural and religious activities; (6) foster and coordinate all efforts in behalf of the health and social welfare of Jews and the relief of suffering and poverty among them; (7) foster cultural creativity by enlisting the service of creative talents to translate Jewish experiences and values into works of art; (8) help Jews meet economic difficulties due to discrimination by both Gentiles and Jews, and defend Jewish rights against encroachment and the Jewish name against defamation; (9) collaborate with all non-Jewish groups and civic movements for the promotion of the common welfare of the general population.

Organic Community should constitute an adaptation of the traditional sense of nationhood, which held the Jews together in the past, to such conditions as obtain under democratic nationalism. The basic need with which communal life should reckon is that of helping the individual Jew overcome, both externally and internally, the difficulties he encounters in his economic, social and cultural life by reason of anti-Semitism.

Whether we like it or not, anti-Semitism will for a long time yet have to be taken into account. Mankind will require considerable re-education to purge itself of the poison of Jew-hatred with which it has been inoculated by the Church. For centuries the Church taught its adherents to regard the Jews as deicides and as the accursed of God. Even when Christianity is superseded by some secular cult, whether it be nationalism or humanism, the prejudice against the Jews continues to smoulder, and it flares up at the least opportunity. Any political or economic crisis is sufficient to awaken that prejudice. Hence, in both normal and abnormal times, Jews must count upon being exposed to the assaults of anti-Semitism.

With anti-Semitism as too brutal a fact to be ignored, and with its destructive and demoralizing influence on the Jews, whom it terrorizes with economic and industrial boycott, no collective effort on the part of Jews can ever gain the support and participation of the masses, unless its primary task be to mitigate the cruel effects of that boycott. In numerous instances, the young people have to deny that they are Jews, or else they would be doomed to starve. Even Jewish employers, fearing to lose customers, if they employed Jews, ask the employment agencies not to send them Jews. The thousands of Jewish young people who find their Jewishness a serious handicap in their careers will not respond to the most strenuous Jewish educational and cultural efforts, unless the Jewish community try to help them overcome that handicap.

The outstanding characteristic of anti-Semitism is that it accentuates "the collective responsibility of the whole Jewish world for every individual Jew. Let an Englishman or a Frenchman come into conflict with the law, and it is one man's affair. But let a Jew come into conflict with the law, and it is *every* Jew's affair. Every Jew must bear the responsibility not only for his own misdeeds, but for those of every other Jew, not only in his own city and country, but in all the cities and countries of the world. . . ." "This is," as Kurt Lewin rightly says, "a responsibility beyond human endurance" (*Cf.* "Bringing Up the Jewish Child," in *Resolving Social Conflicts,* pp. 169-185). The very purpose of organized Jewish life should be, paradoxical as it may seem, at least to relieve the Jewish mind of that unnatural responsibility. Jews are no different from other human beings, and they should not succumb to the self-hatred which is bound to result from the acceptance of this unnatural responsibility. If collective Jewish life were normalized, the sphere of collective responsibility would be clearly defined. Such definition would exempt the Jewish people from any responsibility for things beyond communal control. This would not appease the anti-Semites, but it would set at ease the minds of the Jews.

Although affiliation with the Jewish Community would initially have to be voluntary, once affiliation has taken place, it would have to constitute a commitment and an acceptance of certain rules and regulations without which there can be no organization, to say nothing of *organic* Community. We must therefore expect the Jewish Community to exercise a degree of social authority, particularly in the two following areas: (1) the area of marriage and divorce problems, and (2) the area of minimum moral standards in the dealings of Jews with one another and with non-Jews.

In marriage and divorce, the objective will have to be the retention of the general spirit of marital fidelity emphasized in the Jewish tradition. As for those traditional laws, however, which either work undue hardship on the parties concerned, or which are based on ethical conceptions lower than those which have been achieved by the best part of mankind, new norms should be established and new lines of action adopted. In that way, Judaism as a civilization may contribute to the enhancement of the Jew's

personal life by means not only of its ideals and standards, but
also by its character as the collective expression of the Jewish
People.

*For Jewish peoplehood to play a salvational role in the life
of the individual Jew, it will have to be reconstituted by a public
declaration similar to the Basle Platform.* Such a declaration will
have to be issued by a Jewish World Assembly, representative .of
all shades of opinion in Jewish life, but having one goal in common: the perpetuation of the Jewish People and the maintenance
of its sense of continuity with the People that produced the Bible
and the tradition based on it. Before issuing such a declaration,
the World Assembly will have to confer for a considerable period
of time, and take up the many basic problems of salvation, religion, collective life, and particularly those of nationalism and
socialism which trouble the Jewish People. The most difficult
problem of all which can no longer be evaded is how to deal with
the irreconcilable differences in viewpoint between the Orthodox
and non-Orthodox.

Affirmatively the declaration that is to come forth from the
Jewish World Assembly will have to make clear that Jews throughout the world aim to continue as a People, dedicated to the purpose of helping its members achieve their salvation through furthering the cause of universal freedom, justice and peace, and that,
by being so dedicated, it is furthering the cause of beneficent
religion.

Given this larger perspective, the New Zionism would enable
Judaism, as a religious civilization, to effect the transition from
other-worldliness to this-worldliness. It would help the Jewish
People to meet the challenge of modern nationalism by recognizing
its indispensable role in civilization and impressing it into the
service of human unity. At the same time, it would enable Judaism
to meet the challenge implied in some of the other corollaries of
this-worldly salvation. How it would do that will be discussed in
the next two chapters, which treat of Eretz Yisrael and the Jewish
way of life in terms of this-worldly salvation.

BIBLIOGRAPHY

ERNEST BARKER, *National Character and the Factors in Its Formation*, N. Y., Harper and Brother, 1927.

NAHUM GOLDMANN, *Status of Jewry*, World Jewish Congress, 1953.

MORDECAI M. KAPLAN, "The Status of Jews, The Significance of Being a People, Living in Two Civilizations, Community—The Social Structure of American-Jewish Life," in *The Future of the American Jew*, N. Y., Macmillan, 1947, pp. 58-123.

——. "The Nationhood of Israel, Nationalism as a Cultural Concept, Nationalism as the Call of the Spirit," in *Judaism as a Civilization*, pp. 227-263.

KURT LEWIN, *Resolving Social Conflicts*, N. Y., Harper and Brother, 1948.

JAMES T. SHOTWELL, "The Old Testament as History," in *An Introduction to History*, N. Y., Columbia University Press, 1822, pp. 79-107.

EVERETT V. STONEQUIST, *The Marginal Man*, N. Y., Scribners, 1937.

CHAPTER V

The Reclamation of Eretz Yisrael

I

The centrality of Eretz Yisrael in the destiny of the Jewish People belongs to a thought pattern which antedates even the other-worldly stage of Judaism. The selection of Eretz Yisrael by YHWH, the God of Israel, to be His holy land, set aside for the People He chose to be representative of Man, is part of the central theme of the Torah. The land is holy in a sense that is both more primitive and more advanced than that in which it is holy to Christians and Moslems. For Christians, it is holy mainly as the setting in which Jesus spent the few eventful years of his life. For Moslems, it is holy because it is associated with some miraculous experiences vouchsafed to Mohammed. To the Jews, the land is holy in the sense that, while their entire career as a People is viewed as a revelation of divinity, God's favor is revealed largely by their peaceful and secure possession of the land, and His displeasure by their exile from it. If they lived in fear of enemies without, or were torn by discord within, it was because they had failed to live in accordance with God's law. When the measure of their sin became full, Eretz Yisrael would endure them no longer, but "thrust them out," as it had thrust out the nations that had occupied it before the Israelites took possession of it.

The foregoing view of the land is primitive, because it is associated with a conception of God that circumscribes His Godhood, or His highest love and guidance of human beings, within geographic limits, though it may at the same time affirm His power and dominion as unlimited. Yet, it may be that this view, for want of a more adequate conception, was merely a way of expressing the Jew's own profound attachment to his People. Sensing that the land was an instrument used by God in the molding of the Jewish People, Jews have apotheosized the land. When Jews migrated to it, despite the greatest hardships in reaching it and in living there, they were impelled to endure all these because, in the thought pattern of other-worldly belief, they believed the land could cleanse them of sin and assure them a portion in the world to come.

Does the transition to humanist and this-worldly religion call for the complete repudiation of this attitude toward Eretz Yisrael? Such a proposal would constitute a complete break with the Jewish past. If, as suggested, the traditional attitude toward the land was the pre-modern apotheosis of those instruments which formed and preserved the Jews as a People, it should not be difficult to translate into the key of this-worldliness that love for the land without which it is inconceivable that the Jews can be reconstituted once again into a People.

In his protest against the British Government's 1939 White Paper, Chaim Weizmann said: "We have never relinquished our claim to Palestine. We have never ceased our contact with the country throughout the thousands of years that we have been forcibly separated from it. . . . Jewish life in a minor or major degree has progressed in Palestine throughout the ages. Had it not been for the religious fervor and mystical enthusiasm which permeates every Jew when he toils on the land of Palestine, our pioneers would never have achieved what they have done in Palestine. We can no more foresake our right to Palestine than we can forsake our souls, our religion, our great tradition—a tradition perhaps the oldest among the traditions of civilized nations" (*The Palestine Post,* Friday, June 2, 1939).

If Zionism is to make the reclamation of Eretz Yisrael a moral and spiritual obligation of all Jews, including those who regard Diaspora as a permanent condition of Jewish life, it has to formulate a rationale whereby that obligation can be shown to be part of every Jew's striving to fulfill himself as a human being. "Give us first a stone whereon to lay our head," wrote Berditchewski, "and then we shall dream."

Such an obligation must now be based upon an elaborate rationale instead of on implicit faith, in view of the radical change which has taken place in men's outlook on life. It has become necessary to spell out the duty of reclaiming Eretz Yisrael in terms of this-worldly salvation.

The transition from a mode of human life based on authoritarianism and unquestioning acceptance of an other-worldly pattern of conduct and belief, to one based on self-direction and a critical approach to any proposed this-worldly pattern of destiny is a difficult one to negotiate. It calls for a rationale whereby we might be able to transpose the permanent values of the past into the key of new axiomatic values which the present· time might regard as their equivalent.

The need for articulating a modern rationale for the return to Eretz Yisrael was experienced by the socialists among secular Zionists. They had to defend what was termed "the territorial principle of Zionism" against their Jewish fellow socialists, the members of the *Bund* (League of the Jewish Workingmen of Lithuania, Poland and Russia), who maintained their Jewish nationhood, but saw no need for migrating to Palestine. The chief spokesman among the socialists for a return to Eretz Yisrael was Ber Borochov. He arrived at the territorial principle of Jewish nationhood through his socialist philosophy. He assumed that Jews were destined to be forever barred from the basic industries; they were doomed to a greater degree of insecurity than was the lot of the laboring classes among other peoples. He insisted, contrary to the contention of Marx, Engels and Kautsky, that Jews were discriminated against not as individuals but as a group. Hence they should accept their nationhood and transplant themselves to Palestine, the only territory where they could freely strike root in agriculture, mining and other basic industries.

Whatever truth there may have been in Borochov's analysis of the economic future of the Jews in the Old World, it is doubtful whether it applies to Jews in the New World. Moreover, this kind of rationale for the territorial principle of Zionism suffers from a double weakness: first, it is merely a reaction to a particular situation to which alternative reactions are possible; secondly there

is no need to ground so basic a principle on such a shaky foundation. The centrality of Zion can be established by a rationale
inherent not only in the very nature of Judaism, as the evolving
religious civilization of the Jewish People, but also in the human
nature of the kind of group that consciously seeks to serve as a
means of salvation for its members.

II

The attainment of this-worldly salvation presupposes belonging to a People which provides its members with something more
than a tradition and an authoritative way of life. Such a People
should enable its members not only to interact freely in pursuit
of their everyday interests, but also to derive from their interaction
experiences valuable as means of salvation.

For a People to meet that condition it has to be able to
exercise a large degree of autonomy in a land it can call its own.
For us Jews, Eretz Yisrael in the past was, and must become
again, such a land. Individually, Jews may prosper and enjoy
full political and social equality, no matter how few in number,
wherever they live in free countries. But so long as they constitute
a minority, they can scarcely be in a position to develop fully the
high purposes and ideas implicit in their Jewish heritage. What
happens to Jews, even when well off politically and economically,
in an environment where it is the custom to exploit the depressed
classes, is well illustrated in the case of the South African Jews.
"They were the economic pioneers of South Africa," we are told.
"They introduced merino sheep, cotton and sugar cane and An-
gora goats to start the mohair industry. They started the very
valuable ostrich feather industry. Today there are about 100,000
Jews in the Union, and they, like the two and a half million
Afrikaners and English, believe in the segregation of the Bantus
and have strong social prejudices against non-Europeans (Carveth
Wells in the Saturday Review, on *The South African Way of Life,*
July 10, 1954, edited by G. H. Calpin, N. Y., 1954).

Quite in contrast with the attitude of South African Jews
toward the disinherited classes is that of the Jews in Israel. In a
book in the Afrikaans language entitled "Has the Afrikaner Na-

tion a Future" by G. D. Scholtz, an intransigeant Afrikaner nationalist, the Jews in Israel are held up as an example to the Afrikaner nation of 1,000,000 for having learned to do the hardest work with their own hands and abandoned any dependence on cheap native labor (*Cf.* New York Times, August 31, 1954).

"Does not Judaism's dependence upon an autonomous group life in a land of its own," one may ask, "reduce Judaism to a type of national religious civilization? Such civilizations prevailed before the rise of world religions like Christianity and Islam, but are they not outdated in our time?" The fact, however, is that national religious civilizations are the inevitable outcome of the new direction which man's search for salvation has taken. It should therefore not be surprising if modern nationalism returns, on a higher and more inclusive level, to the kind of religion that produced the Bible. *That is the kind of religion which is land-rooted in content, but universal in form and reference.*

Everyone of the "Fathers of modern nationalism"—Rousseau, Burke, Mazzini, Fichte and Jefferson—envisaged for his own People some form of religion that would express its native genius, and be integral to its intrinsic culture or civilization. Virtually all of them drew upon the Jewish Scriptures for the type of religion in which their vision of a new national life for their peoples was to find expression. The resurgence of national religion may be discerned in the way patriotism has been developed within the last two centuries from a questionable virtue to a veritable religious cult.

On the other hand, hardly anything in the modern world gives men greater concern than the ruthless inhumanity into which modern nationalism can degenerate when it falls into the hands of power-mad leaders. For that reason any religion, or religious civilization, that wishes to serve mankind must first of all impose moral restraint upon national patriotisms, and guide them into a universal internationalism that would aim to establish freedom, justice and peace in the world.

For those who still subscribe to supernaturalistic or otherworldly religion, whether Jews, Christians or Moslems, there is enough in it, if activated, to counteract the fanatical drive of national patriotism. But for the growing number of those to whom that kind of religion has become meaningless, there is great danger that the vacuum will be filled by some kind of bureaucratic totalitarianism of an economic or nationalist type. *Thus, what Jews have to evolve, in order to give meaning to their lives in a complex society, may point the way to a solution of the dilemma presented by modern patriotism.*

III

In resuming a national life in Eretz Yisrael, the land that embodies its highest aspirations, Judaism demonstrates the principle that it is normal for religion to convert into means of salvation the experiences arising from the social interaction which a common land makes necessary for a People. The organic collective life resulting from the common interests which people, living in close proximity, must of necessity share is, despite the philosophy of existentialism, more existentially real and certainly of far longer duration than any individual member of the group, however great. Even the most distinguished individual is far more in debt to his society than it is to him. Thus a territorial society provides what every man needs for his salvation, and is the initial source of his experiencing the meaning of Godhood.

How readily Jewish national life in Israel can give rise to new cultural and spiritual values is evidenced by the practice, instituted there recently, of using the celebration of Independence Day as an occasion for Israel Awards to scholars, scientists and men of letters in recognition of distinguished work in their various fields. That work embraces poetry, fiction, music, natural and exact science, philosophy, law, education and Bible studies (*Israel Digest,* May 17, 1954).

Jews who live in the Diaspora, by maintaining their oneness with the Jews in Eretz Yisrael, may serve to restrain the chauvinistic tendencies which the Israeli struggle for survival is apt to produce. On the other hand, they will also participate in the experiences of the Jews in Eretz Yisrael, together with the moral and spiritual values which those experiences may yield. We need only recall how closely the average American Jew at present fol-

lows the daily events in Israel and how sensitive he is to what
goes on there. How long that interest will continue—that is the
problem. "The bond with the Jewish People wherever they may
live is the solid foundation of our life," declared Prime Minister
Moshe Sharett, "just as the spiritual attachment to the State of
Israel is the central fact in the life of the Jewish People" (*Ibid.*
May 17, 1954). Sharett speaks advisedly of the attachment to
the State of Israel as "spiritual."

If world Jewry will reconstitute itself as a People and achieve
a modern national civilization in Eretz Yisrael and a religious
cultural life everywhere, it will place itself in the vanguard of an
urgently needed new trend in world civilization, already becoming
manifest in the more advanced nations of the Western world. On
the one hand, they utilize their own historic experiences and their
own *sancta* (such as their great personalities, their memorable
events and places) as sources of morale and guidance, and on
the other hand, they seek to integrate their own collective interests, both material and spiritual, within the common life of mankind. Without such integration, which only the acceptance of some
kind of universal religion can make possible, mankind will revert
to nationalist idolatry, with all its excesses.

Thus in treating the reclamation of Eretz Yisrael as part of
a modern messianic or religious movement, Jews have a unique
opportunity to serve mankind by fostering a method of group life
directed towards this-worldly salvation. This achievement will justify
the age-old refusal of the Jewish People to renounce Eretz Yisrael.
When, in an historic demonstration of unexampled loyalty, the
East European Zionists rejected the offer of Uganda as a national
territory, *they proved that the Zionist movement was basically
motivated by Jewish cultural nationalism, with its roots in the
Jewish tradition, rather than by modern political nationalism.*

The mistake of the Reform Movement, in its initial stage,
was not in maintaining that the Jews have a universal mission.
Whenever we try to live a useful and meaningful life, we exert
a beneficent influence. If, as a group, we make this our deliberate
purpose, we may be said to have a mission. The mistake of the
Reform Movement consisted in having expected the Jews to do

what the Talmud describes as "breaking the cask without spilling the wine." Although the leaders of the Movement consented to the fragmentation of the Jewish People and the renunciation of its homeland, they nevertheless expected the Jews as a group to influence all mankind to accept the fatherhood of God and the brotherhood of man. Those leaders made little, if any effort, to indicate what Jews were expected to do, or live up to, in order that they might fulfill so high a mission. They seem to have believed that, if the Jews kept on affirming as emphatically as possible that they had been chosen for that mission, it would somehow get itself fulfilled.

On the other hand, the particularity of a group does not prevent it from developing ways of living and spiritual values capable of being universalized and of stimulating other groups to creativity. The idea of such universal life values is implicit in the form of the Jewish People's attachment to Eretz Yisrael; it must now be made explicit. The process of realizing such values consists in utilizing for self-fulfillment as human beings that wide range of interactivity which is possible only among those who are rooted in a common land. *Earthly interests must constitute the stuff out of which human beings may mold their destiny. That is the Jewish contribution to the method of salvation whose source and guarantor is God.*

To demonstrate the validity of that method of salvation, Judaism needs a home: that is, a land where Jews, as the majority population, can demonstrate how a People may make its civilization an instrument for the maximum human self-fulfillment of its individual members. There is a spiritual advantage in "being true to a particular piece of earth—true to its landscape, its climate, its history, its morality, its tongue."

Only in such a land can enough members of a People live in that propinquity which necessitates interaction in pursuit of common economic, social and political interests. Only such interaction provides that inexhaustible flow of new experience without which cultural, moral and spiritual values are void of content. Only in such a context can develop the freedom which has been defined as "that faculty of man by which he is able to determine his being through history" (Tillich). *Eretz Yisrael is indispensable to Jews as the realm of freedom to be creative as Jews.* Only thus can the Jewish People make history, instead of being its passive product.

After all is said and done, if it were not for the unparalleled attachment of the Jewish People to Eretz Yisrael, and the inexhaustible meanings for human life that have derived for all mankind from that attachment, the resentment of the Arab world at the Zionist movement would be at least understandable, even if not justified. There can be no question that, without our historic claim to the land, the nations, including Britain, would never have made it possible for Jews to rebuild it as their homeland and ultimately to establish there a political state.

The Arab nations destroyed any possible justification for their anti-Zionism when they flouted the final decision of the United Nations to restore to the Jews at least part of their ancient land. Reasonable in itself, that solution was the only way the civilized nations had to make amends for having passively looked on while Hitler and his myrmidons were massacring millions of Jews. That brutal genocide could be perpetrated on so vast a scale only because of the heartless failure of the democratic nations, which were brought together before World War II at the conference in Evian, to offer refuge to the Jews who were hit by Hitler's Nuremberg laws.

It therefore devolves upon the Zionist movement, in its effort to reconstitute the Jewish People and arouse in Diaspora Jewry a sense of personal involvement in the consolidation of the State of Israel, to develop fully the far-reaching religious, or salvational, implications of our historical claim to the land of Israel. From the very beginning Zionism presented itself as not merely a movement to salvage human lives, desperately urgent as that was, but as seeking to resurrect a People that had made history and evolved moral and spiritual values which half of mankind have incorporated into their consciousness and made part of their conscience.

IV

Jewish history and values are the product of the interaction between the Jewish People and Eretz Yisrael. *World Jewry without Eretz Yisrael is like a soul without a body; Eretz Yisrael without World Jewry is like a body without a soul.*

The interplay of people and land is more responsible for the individuality of the Jewish People and its contribution to civilization than any other factor in its life, be it even its tradition, or its outstanding spiritual leaders. Those leaders themselves were the product of that interrelationship between land and people, in terms of which they guided, warned and comforted their contemporaries. That interplay of land and people is without parallel in human history; a fact that has been accepted as fundamental to religion, and which has made Eretz Yisrael a Holy Land for half of mankind. The effort to resume the interaction of the Jewish People with its land cannot succeed if it ignores this.

Zionist leaders should possess the moral courage to present the Zionist movement as a messianic movement to world Jewry. In Jewish tradition, the Messiah represents the reawakening of the Jewish People to a sense of destiny and the resumption of Jewish nationhood in the land of its origin and development. Even in its traditional setting, Messianism belongs to a different dimension from that of other-worldliness. It was conceived as breaking through the bonds of the natural order, but not as destroying it, as inaugurating a new era in the life of mankind and culminating in the rise of a free People, re-wedded to its soil and giving birth to the new man. The twice-told Messianic prophecy that "in the end of days" peace will reign throughout the world and men "will not learn war anymore," is certainly a promise for this, our world.

Such Messianism is of the very essence of Jewish religion. Zionism must make Jews everywhere take Messianism seriously and translate it into religion. In no other way can Zionism make American Jews treat as a moral and religious responsibility the recruitment of *halutzim* to help build the land, and develop all forms of personal involvement in its security and in the achievement of its high purposes. Referring to the sudden change of habits which modern conditions often demand, Karl Mannheim writes: "It can only take place, if enthusiasm or an emotionalization of the new issues accompanies it, and the latter occurs only when the crucial issues of life can be re-defined and gain new significance . . . this general revaluation can only happen if each new objective is part of a new world view and a new way of life" (*Diagnosis of Our Time*, p. 115).

Zionism at long last must do what Judah Halevi, many centuries ago, urged Jews to do. It should put an end to the habit of treating the role which Eretz Yisrael played in the past, and which it is destined to play in the future, as no more than a thema for liturgy. More than ever has it became necessary for Zionism to enlarge its perspective. One of its main purposes should be to deepen our awareness of the extent to which the Jewish being was fashioned by Eretz Yisrael. Zionism should stress that during the centuries of their dispersion Eretz Yisrael played a greater role in the spiritual life of the Jews than the countries which they actually inhabited.

Zionism should urge Jews to read their tradition with fresh eyes. If Jews were to do so, they would discover that they have in the Pentateuch—the basic source of the sanctions, laws, and folkways of the Jewish People—a perfectly recorded deed to the eternal possession of Eretz Yisrael. Moreover, it is stated there in bold and unmistakable terms that even if the children of Israel will be exiled from the land, they will not entirely forfeit it, but that ultimately their descendants will return to it, and rebuild their national life.

V

In reemphasizing the centrality of Eretz Yisrael in Judaism, the New Zionism should be prepared to counter two possible objections that may present themselves.

First, there is the contention that identifying a religion with a particular land was normal in ancient times, when each land was for those who lived in it all that constituted what was worthwhile in the world. Hence each land was to its inhabitants the

special possession of their god or gods. Though the Jews ascribed
to their God universal dominion, they, nevertheless, deemed themselves a chosen and privileged People. They thus ascribed to their
religion an exclusiveness inconsistent with the conception of God
as ruler of mankind, and with the idea that all lands offer adequate opportunities to their inhabitants to achieve salvation.

Though that objection might have been valid before the rise
of Christianity and Islam, it has lost all effect, since the history
of the Jewish People in Eretz Yisrael has come to figure in the
conscience of mankind as evidence of God's self-revelation through
human history. That history has helped to redirect men's search
for God. Instead of expecting God to manifest Himself in the
phenomena of nature, men discern in the moral and spiritual
forces which make for justice and loving-kindness as manifestations
of Godhood.

That unique reading of history as the revelation of God transcends the bounds of the Jewish People in its significance, despite its indissoluble bonds with Eretz Yisrael. Eretz Yisrael has
come to be a Holy Land for all nations who look to the Jewish
heritage as the source of their religion. Whatever constricting influence association with a particular land may originally have had
on Jewish religion, it can have no contemporary significance in
view of the role of the Jewish religion in the rise of Christianity
and Islam. Had Jewish religion inherently been narrowly national
or land-bound, it could never have given rise to those two world
religions.

The foregoing facts also help us meet a second objection to
the reclamation of Eretz Yisrael as a religiously significant act,
namely, that the original conquest of the land bears the stigma
of violence. Such a movement should be free of all taint of violence, no matter at how remote a past that taint entered.

As is well-known, Jewish tradition displays a strong sensitivity
on that point. Its answer is that ancient Israel's invasion of the
land was not an act of *force majeure*. The ancient Israelites never
possessed enough force for that. Only through obedience to the
will of God and with His aid, did they take possession of the land.

Can this traditional interpretation be transposed into the terms of our present day sense of justice? Had there been successors to the aborigines of Eretz Yisrael to demand the return of the land to them, tradition or no tradition, we Jews would not, in justice, be able to advance our claim to the land. But with no aboriginal peoples to contest the Jewish claim, and considering the great moral and spiritual heritage which our ancestors developed in Eretz Yisrael and our own passionate sincerity in resuming the responsibility for creating an exemplary kind of life there, *the fact that it was originally acquired by force has been erased from the books of account which record the God-revealing history of the Jewish People.*

The fact that the foregoing argument is evidently apologetic does not invalidate it. This is not the kind of special pleading ordinarily devised by publicists or theologians, in attempting to make the worse cause appear the better. It is merely a continuation of an ethical position which the conscience of the ancient Israelites themselves formulated. We are aided in understanding that fact and appreciating its ethical significance by the modern evolutionary conception of the Torah and of ancient Jewish religion. For in the light of critical analysis, the explanation which the Torah gives for the dispossession of the natives of Canaan by the Israelites came a long time after the event. This implies that at the time the Israelites invaded Canaan they were dominated by the usual rapacious drive that periodically sent hungry Bedouins out in search of fertile territory. But as their ethical conscience developed over the centuries, and they contemplated in retrospect their invasion of the land, they gave it the apologetic form which is presented in the Torah. That version became the basis of the entire ethico-religious thought pattern of Judaism. It did not remain merely a literary or theological conceit; it made history. That *history* is the sound moral foundation of the Jewish claim to Eretz Yisrael.

VI

Nevertheless, no apologetic nor historic claim, be it ever so valid, would by itself be sufficient to confirm the Jews' right to Eretz Yisrael. A more convincing argument is needed, an argument not of words but of deeds, such as the work of reclaiming the land from its ruinous and sterile condition, and converting it from the disease-ridden country that it was in the past, for its limited and static population, into a land that is healthily habitable and productive for a growing population that is far from having reached its limit. A few of the facts and figures quoted in an address by Ben Gurion at an Extraordinary Zionist Conference in New York, on May 12, 1942, tell the story of what the Zionist *argument of works* has in large measure achieved.

According to a public statement made by the Arab delegates at the London Palestine Conference in 1939, there were in the whole Western Palestine only seven and a half million ˙dunams (about two million acres) of cultivable land. The whole area of the country then amounted to twenty-six and a half million dunam. Thus according to the Arabs, some nineteen million dunam were uncultivable and were certainly not cultivated by the Arabs. "Practice has shown," adds Ben Gurion, *"that what is uncultivated and considered uncultivable by the Arabs is cultivable and has been cultivated by Jews."* He mentions the sands of Rishon Letzion, the swamps of Hedera, the rocks of Motza, the stony hills of Hanita and—the most conspicuous example—the largest malarial area in Palestine, the Huleh Basin.

"Jews had not merely to acquire land but to reclaim, drain, reforest, fertilize and, wherever water could be discovered, irrigate it. In this way, and by the introduction of modern and intensive methods of cultivation, modern machinery, new breeds of cattle and poultry, new plants and seeds, rotation of crops, and by utilizing surface and sub-soil water to the best advantage, they made land available for settlement."

The electrification of the country and the exploitation of raw materials, particularly the chemical riches of the Dead Sea, were made possible by Jewish initiative, capital investment and energy. The Dead Sea works have been seriously hampered, unfortunately,

by the aftermath of Arab-Jewish war, but new sources of raw
material, oil and minerals, are being energetically sought. In the
meantime, much effort and capital have gone into the building
of industries and the establishment of urban centers. The geographic position of Eretz Yisrael gives it a high potential of economic development not only industrial, but also commercial, by
taking advantage of the trade routes of the Mediterranean and
the Red Sea. "Jews went back to the soil," said Ben Gurion,
"they are also going back to the sea."

Long before Jews achieved in Eretz Yisrael what they have
since the establishment of the State of Israel, Dorothy Thompson,
in an address on March 21, 1944, evaluated the significance of
the rebuilding of Eretz Yisrael for world civilization. "Only the
Lord of Creation will save Jewry," she said, "He who is the God
of Love to those who keep His commandments. The Jews of Zion
have kept His commandments. What indifference and waste have
taken from His Earth they have replaced. What ignorance and
greed have neglected, they have supplied. And as long as they
keep on building, as long as the creative spirit moves them in their
great trek toward Palestine, he who stands in the way is halting
the whole progress of man into the only true liberation: Liberation is work, and sweat, for the building of new homes, new
cities, new civilizations, for and by the outcasts and the unwanted
of the earth" (*Jewish Frontier Anthology,* p. 130).

*For us Jews, the upbuilding of Eretz Yisrael is more than
liberation. It is religion in action.* It is as such that the New Zionism should interpret a creative effort sponsored by a People, and
not merely by a State. That is what is needed today to resurrect
the spirit of *halutziut.* Eretz Yisrael cannot be adequately and
properly rebuilt without pioneering men and women. They will
have to come to Eretz Yisrael, particularly from the free countries
of the world, and resume the task of building the land in the
spirit of the early pioneers.

There could not have been any State of Israel without the
foundation laid by the toil, sweat and blood of those pioneers.
The influx of a large immigrant population to whom Eretz Yisrael
was merely a haven of refuge created conditions which have

dampened the early pioneering enthusiasm. The growth of cities and the expansion of industry, with the temptations to slackness arising from an easier flow of goods and services, has put a heavy strain on the spontaneous zeal and spirit of sacrifice which the reclamation of Eretz Yisrael elicited. Actually even in Israel, *halut-ziut* has lost its former drive. That is evident in the reluctance of youth to respond to the call to establish colonies in the Negev.

American Jews have a sufficiently large number of young people who possess the hardihood, idealism and courage to be *halutzim*. Whenever there presented itself a cause which stirred sufficiently their ethical or spiritual imagination they were quick to respond. The recruits to the Jewish Legion organized by Jabotinsky, the large numbers who joined the Loyalists in the Spanish Civil War, and those who came from overseas to help the Jews in their war against the Arabs, are a sufficient indication of the presence of pioneer material among American Jews. What is needed is a cause capable of stirring them to action. The present decline in the spirit of *halutziut* in Israel itself should convince Zionists of the need of some strong inner drive within Jewish life itself. That inner drive need be none other than the one that once aroused the Biluim, and the successive *aliyot,* or waves of immigration, to seek in Eretz Yisrael their own self-fulfillment through dedicating themselves to the remaking of their People and the reclamation of its land.

VII

A most remarkable demonstration of the role played by a land in generating an ethico-spiritual religion, such as Jewish religion will evolve into, if once again reunited with Eretz Yisrael, is the "Unspoken National Faith" of the American people. In an article explaining "Why Americans need no ideology," Daniel J. Boorstin points to the fact that the American people has something of more significance and profounder than an ideology ("Our Unspoken National Faith," *Commentary,* April 1953). It has what he calls a "national faith" which, though unrecognized and "unspoken," he delineates as constituting a national religion, grounded in the realities of the specific history and geography of the United

States. Though in describing that faith, the author is concerned
mainly with its political implications, particularly with the un-
likelihood that the United States would ever come to adopt either
Communist or Fascist ideologies, he actually outlines a kind of
modern religious civilization in the making. Judaism will have to
become that kind of a primary religious civilization for Jews in
Eretz Yisrael and a secondary one for Jews in the Diaspora.

The Jews of the United States are thus in the favorable position of being able to find in the American civilization, which must
necessarily be their primary one, the first large scale application
of the spiritual method underlying their own Jewish civilization.
That large scale application is at present still undefined. That it
has taken a Jew to identify the spiritual method that American
civilization shares with Jewish is, indeed, significant. But the first
deliberate application of that method, on the part of Jews, will
have to take place in Eretz Yisrael. Otherwise, it is questionable
whether anything will survive of Judaism or of the Jewish People,
except for a fossilized Orthodoxy.

Just what is the "Unspoken National Faith" of the American
People, which, according to Boorstin, contains both promise and
validation of a land-rooted religious civilization, and which it
should be Zionism's task to foster in and outside Israel? In substance, it is the following:

First, the American nation believes that it has received its
ideals "as a gift from the *past*." It assumes that the earliest settlers
or Founding Fathers equipped it with a way of life adequate to
all its future needs. That induces the American nation "to draw
heavily on the materials of its history, but always in a distinctly
non-historical frame of mind." Boorstin compares this idea to the
obsolete biological notion of "pre-formation," or the notion that
all parts of an organism pre-exist in perfect miniature in the seed.
Similarly, Americans seem to believe that, if they could understand the ideas of the Pilgrim Fathers or Founding Fathers, they
would find "the perfect embryo of the theory by which we now
live." That accounts for the American Constitution and the way
it is interpreted. "Changes in our policy or our institutions are
read back into the ideas and sometimes into the very words of

the Founding Fathers." This has actually in one sense made the Federal Constitution an "unwritten document." "The unique role," wites Boorstin, "which our national past has played in constructing our image of ourselves ànd our standards for American life has made us hypersensitive about our history."

The resemblance between, on the one hand, the rootedness of the American way of life in their historic past and Constitutional tradition, and on the other, of the Jewish way of life in the past of the Jewish People and in the Torah, on which the Jews have drawn "in a distinctly non-historical frame of mind," is too evident to need laboring.

A second characteristic of American civilization which has its parallel in Jewish civilization is "the remarkable continuity or homogeneity of American history . . . in contrast with the discontinuity of European history." That seems paradoxical at first sight, but actually it is not surprising when we realize that, though the European peoples are older than the American, their civilizations consist of many layers. The topmost nationalist one, which is of immediate relevance to contemporary problems, is still in its initial stage. Their history is anything but homogeneous. For Boorstin, that fact explains in part why Americans find no need to follow the European style of world betterment. "People all over Europe," he says, "have become accustomed, during the last century, to the notion that man can better his condition by trying to remake his institutions in some colossal image. Fascism and Nazism proposed this; and so does Communism. Europe has not yet realized that the remedy it seeks is itself a disease. . . . In contrast with this . . . is the axiom that institutions are not and should not be the grand creations of men toward large' ends and outspoken values; rather they are organisms which grow out of the soil in which they are rooted and out of the tradition from which they have sprung."

In this we have an intimation of what a People achieves through the continuity or homogeneity of its history. It is enabled to adjust itself creatively to changing conditions, without the violence of bloody revolutions and the subsequent tyranny which alone prevents those revolutions from turning into mutual

slaughter. But the advantage of historic continuity is not merely
negative. Its positive aspect is, surely, a deepened love and de-
votion to the People and its way of life, tantamount to a national
faith or religion. A consecrated way of life, or civilization, is religious, whether or not it is identified as such, whether or not it
has specific rituals by which its religious character is rendered
conspicuous. From this significant parallel, in the matter of historic continuity, between the two civilizations, the American and
the Jewish, Zionism might learn what it has to do to develop
Erezt Yisrael as the home of a Jewish religious civilization.

The most important lesson, however, which Zionism may
well derive from America's "unspoken national faith" is the religious significance of the enduring stamp impressed upon the
American People by its earliest history, and by the historic continuity made possible through "the American landscape." "The
idea that the American landscape is a giver of values," writes
Boorstin, "is, of course, old and familiar. It has long been believed
that, in America, the community's values . . . would somehow be
the gift of the continent itself." In American patriotism, the land
is viewed as a source of mystical power. "We have looked anxi-
ously for some common faith," adds Boorstin. "A few writers,
like Louis Adamic, have even tried to make the motleyness itself
a scheme of values: to make the patchwork seem the pattern.
But the readiest solution, a necessary solution, perhaps the only
possible solution for us, has been to assume, in the immigrants'
own phrase, that ours is a 'golden land,' that values spring from
our common ground. If American ideals are not in books or in
the blood, but in the air, then they are readily acquired."

The main advantage, however, which, according to Boorstin,
Americans derive from their attachment to the national landscape
is that, in the process of meeting the changing conditions of life,
they do not have to depend upon supermen, fanatical agitators
and erratic geniuses. "The character of our national heroes bears
witness to . . . our preference for the man who seizes the God-
given opportunities over him who pursues a great private vision."

We thus have in a People's identification with a land not
only the source of its vitality and its faith, but also its means of

adjusting itself to change, however sudden or violent, with a naturalness and ease that render adjustment creative and pro gressive, and enable the People to be a humanizing force in the lives of its members. Thus, both as a means of giving Jewish civilization the vitality which comes only from religion, and of enabling that civilization to reinterpret and reconstruct its traditional values, in keeping with what seems best and truest in the contemporary climate of opinion, Eretz Yisrael, as the ancestral home of Judaism, has to be reclaimed and made productive. All attempts at reconstructing Jewish life and thought apart from the land have some value, insofar as they at least prevent Jewish civilization from losing all capacity for renewal and becoming entirely obsolete. But that kind of Jewish survival is a "medicated survival." It is not a creative survival.

Thus only by viewing the return of the Jewish People to Eretz Yisrael in the context of the life of mankind, and from the standpoint of the past of our People wherein the foundation was laid for a meaningful conception of human existence, can that enterprise assume the importance, and have the impact, of a creative and beneficent religious movement. Against that version of Zionism, no one would dare to voice the petty counter-claim of double loyalty. For that verslon of Zionism many a gifted Jew would be willing to sacrifice ease and comfort to help build the land that now can make good what it has hitherto only been capable of promising.

Herzl defined Zionism as "the Jewish nation on the way." According to Ben Gurion, Zionism is "the Jewish People on its way back to the land." According to the new version of Zionism, it is the remaking of the Jewish People through the remaking of its land.

BIBLIOGRAPHY

BAKER BROWNELL, *The Human Community*, N. Y., 1950.

MARTIN BUBER, *Israel and Palestine*, London, 1952.

MORDECAI M. KAPLAN, "The Land of Israel" in *Judaism as a Civilization*, N. Y., 1934, Chapter XX.

——. "The Role of Eretz Yisrael in the Life of Diaspora Jewry" in *The Future of the American Jew*, N. Y., 1948, Part I, Chapter 7.

BERL LOCKER, *The Jews and Palestine, Historical Connection and Historic Right*, 1938.

WALTER CLAY LOWDERMILK, *Palestine, Land of Promise*, N. Y., 1944.

CHAPTER VI
The Creative Expansion of Torah

I

Zionism, as a movement to redeem the Jewish People and regenerate its spirit through the reconstitution of Jewish Peoplehood and the reclamation of Eretz Yisrael, has to meet the following requirements: (a) it has to foster among the Jews both of Israel and of the Diaspora a sense of interdependence and a process of interaction; and, (b) it has to give the individual Jew the feeling that participating in that interdependence and interaction makes him more of a person. Thus is Zionism to make the Jewish People a means of salvation to the individual Jew. To become that kind of a People is what the Jewish People has to live for. Otherwise its collective survival would become an end in itself. No society which makes survival an end in itself is capable of surviving severe crises.

While the establishment of the State of Israel was the immediate and inevitable objective of Zionism, the problem which now presents itself is: how shall the maintenance of that State be made part of the general purpose for which the Jewish People is to live—namely, the salvation of the individual Jew, whether he live in Israel or elsewhere. The type of state which Jews have to make of Israel is of concern both to the Orthodox and to the non-Orthodox. The Orthodox would mold it as a theocracy, on lines similar to those of Catholic states like Spain and Italy, the non-Orthodox, on lines like those of United States, where half of world Jewry lives today. A similar situation to Israel's exists at present (1954) in Pakistan, which was established in 1947. One clause already adopted in the partly completed constitution specifies that

Pakistan, which has a predominantly Moslem population, shall be governed in accordance with "the democratic principles of the Koran, the Moslem holy book."

Zionism can no longer evade the issue. The only possible solution, if the overwhelming majority of Jews who are non-Orthodox are to be considered, is the separation of the Rabbinate from the State. In this way the Orthodox would have full freedom to live in accordance with the dictates of their conscience, but they would not be able to impose their will on the rest of the community. Nothing can be done about conflicts that involve basic value systems, except to persuade those who live by those systems to let each other alone. It would be even better if they could be made to see the futility and sinfulness of forcing their views on those unable to accept them.

This, however, does not solve the problem of Zionism for the non-Orthodox. If the average individual is to be motivated to invest his life in the future of the Jewish People—which future is to be assured by Zionism—he will have to be appealed to on other grounds than implicit faith in Jewish tradition, or chauvinist loyalty to it. The unorthodox Jew—his number is legion—will not endure the oppressive sense of carrying a barren inheritance. He will expect to find the Jewish People worthy of that investment, not because of any supernatural distinction, nor because of racial superiority, but mainly because it can show itself capable of developing further its historic religious civilization, in response to the intellectual, moral and spiritual needs of our day. The disintegration of the Jewish way of life has resulted in a state of "anomie," which Durkheim defined as "a disintegrated state of society that possesses no body of common values or morals that effectively govern conduct." Only by providing such a "body of common values or morals" can the Jewish way of life prove adequate to the individual Jew and supply him the morale and faith he has to draw upon in his striving for salvation.

The non-Orthodox Zionists are thus confronted with a dilemma. On the one hand, they will not concede to the Rabbinate, or any other religious body, political authority in the Government of Israel. And on the other hand, they cannot maintain the con-

tinuity of Judaism as a religious civilization without religion as
an integral part of Jewish public life. There is no third alternative. They have to find a way of imbuing the Jewish community
in Israel, which is to be the hub of the Jewish People throughout
the world, with the spirit of religion without being theocratic.
That is a problem which can be solved only by the collective
thinking of the best Jewish minds and warmest Jewish hearts,
after long and careful deliberation. At this point we can merely
indicate the direction which their deliberations would be likely
to take.

The task facing Zionism at the present time, in addition to
reconstituting Jewish Peoplehood and reclaiming Eretz Yisrael,
is to enlarge the scope and deepen the meaning of the traditional
concept of Torah. Traditionally, Torah has been understood as
the supernaturally revealed way of life, and its scope was limited
to whatever could come within the frame of that meaning. Henceforth, however, *Torah will have to encompass every phase of
Jewish life and thought, from the standpoint of its bearing on
what has always been the main function of Torah—namely, the
salvation of man.* By relating the satisfaction of life's basic drives,
the physiological and the social, to the supreme need of achieving
the maximum human potential, life comes to be lived in a religious spirit. The purpose of Torah can never become outdated.
To be successful as a means, however, Torah must advance with
the progress of human life. Modern Judaism demands freedom
to search more deeply and to understand more realistically than
was possible in the past what constitutes salvation.

If we are to enlarge the scope of Torah, in the spirit of the
verse "He magnifieth Torah and enhanceth it," we have to widen
its traditional perspective. Torah should henceforth embrace that
aspect of Jewish life which is traditionally designated as *derekh
eretz. The two principal connotations of* derekh eretz *are: "secular interests" and "ethical interests." These have to be made to
figure in Torah to the same degree that they figure in actual life,
and thus to become part of religion as a way of life.*

Our first task is to identify the pragmatic implications of
Torah, or the specific ways in which it has functioned hitherto

in the Jewish consciousness. The next step is to ignore those implications which have become obsolete and to elaborate and implement the rest. There are, in fact, only two implications which have become obsolete: (a) that the Pentateuch, or the Torah of Moses, is a supernaturally dictated text, and (b) that it alone is the final source of whatever is authoritative in Jewish life, whether in terms of law or of social control. On the other hand, there are far more relevant implications than obsolete ones.

The very existence of an "Oral Torah" alongside the "Written Torah" implies the need for conceiving Torah not as a static code, but as an expression of the dynamic process of spiritual growth, through adjustment to new realms of thought and action. That adjustment was regarded in the past as sanctioned by the tradition itself. It was, however, to a larger extent actually dictated by the urgent need to arrive at some *modus vivendi* which submitted to the irresistible demand for change while maintaining the illusion of keeping the tradition unchanged.

The novelty of the human situation in which Jews find themselves precludes the possibility of finding in Torah tradition authoritative guidance in many problems of ritual observance in a manner compatible with what has come to be regarded as a livable way of life. The approach to Torah proposed by Yeshaia Leibovitz of Jerusalem is untenable. On the one hand, he recognizes that the problems of modern living are without precedent, and on the other, he calls upon the Orthodox Rabbinate to find in the Torah tradition precedents on which to base necessary changes in the Law. Nor can modern ethical considerations be weighed merely in terms of ethical values found in the tradition. Leibovitz himself makes that point with regard to the lack of a traditional criterion by which to judge the Kibya incident (*Torah Umitzvot Bazeman Hazeh,* Tel-Aviv, 1954, p. 168). "A group," we are told, "whose culture fails notably to elicit its individual members' possibilities of development, or a group that handicaps its more highly developed members by extreme isolation, must be judged inadequate to their needs" (D. W. Harding, *Social Psychology and Individual Values,* Hutchinson's University Library, London, 1953, p. 67).

II

The only way to maintain the dynamic character of Torah is to identify as Torah whatever affirmative implications of that concept are still valid, and to legislate, educate, and order our lives generally as Jews in the spirit of those implications. "Torah" should not be understood merely as a name for a particular text or collection of texts, or for specific precepts and teachings. It should henceforth denote the entire content of the Jewish religious civilization as a living ongoing process. Likewise, the study of Torah should be conceived as synonymous with life-long education for human self-fulfillment or salvation.

Torah is one of those terms which belong more properly to the predicate of a sentence than to the subject, because it predicates quality like the term "right" or "good." The only way in which we can know fully what it means is by inverting the most significant statements about it, and using it in the predicative sense. We thus get the functional significance of Torah by inverting the verse Psalm 19:8 to read: "Whatever is perfect and restores the soul is the Torah of the Lord."

The predicative sense of Torah is recognizable in a statement like the following: "Even ordinary conversation among Jews is Torah" (Mid. Tehilim 104:3). Perhaps this is what Franz Rosenzweig meant by what he called the "new learning." "It is a learning in reverse order," he writes, "a learning that no longer starts from the Torah and leads into life, but the other way round; from life, from a world that knows nothing of the Law, or pretends to know nothing, back to the Torah. That is the sign of the time" (Glatzer, *Franz Rosenzweig*, p. 231). He credits Buber with developing the principle that Jewish learning has to be understood in such a way that "nothing Jewish is alien" (*Ibid.*, 235).

We may well equate the study of Torah with Plato's conception of education. "Those who are rightly educated generally become good men," says Plato, ". . . It is the first and fairest thing that the best of men can ever have, and which, though liable to take a wrong direction, is capable of reformation. And this work of reformation is the great business of every man while he lives" (*Laws*, 644).

We deliberately introduce this passage from Plato's *Laws* for two reason. First, we wish to suggest that broadening the concept of Torah implies among other things realizing that we Jews have no monopoly on the wisdom of life. On the contrary, the wisdom which we should display as synonymous with Torah should consist in our learning from the wisdom of all peoples, both ancient and modern, acquired by them in the course of their striving for the fulfillment of human destiny. Plato, for example, in the same context from which the above passage is quoted, identifies human fulfillment with "the ideal perfection of citizenship." The traditional Torah, on the other hand, addresses itself to Israel with the precept "Thou shalt be perfect with the Lord thy God."

Secondly, we wish to give Torah a connotation of directed growth and development. That is an idea or value which is lacking in our tradition. The capacity to be self-critical, to recognize that Torah or education may have taken "a wrong direction," and that "*this work of reformation is the business of every man while he lives,*" *is essential not only as a means of regenerating the tradition, but also of perpetuating it. As a tradition succeeds in reforming or reconstructing itself to meet new needs of man, it acquires a new lease on life.*

All this seems entirely remote from what the average Jew associates with the concept Torah, as a result of his hearing the Torah read in the synagogue as part of religious worship. Yet upon reflection, all this is what the ritual of Torah reading should symbolize. The spirit which should accompany the Torah reading on Sabbaths and festivals is beautifully set forth in the following: "We should conceive of Torah reading as a ritual of learning, as a symbol of our reverence for knowledge, our passion for truth seeking, our consuming conviction that knowledge, not ignorance, is the road to bliss and the pathway to God. We should attend it with such instruction as will make it clear that this is an unfinished book, its meaning changing with the changing hungers of men, its pages ever open to new insights" (Jacob J. Weinstein, "The Return to Religion," *Proceedings, Central Conference of American Rabbis Year Book,* 1952, p. 304).

Torah denotes not only a written text but a way of life. As such it deals with those needs of human life which have to be met, if man is to become fully human. Those needs are the following: *To be God-conscious, fellow-man-conscious, and world-conscious.* In identifying them we become aware of their interdependence and of the frustration that is bound to result from the failure to take all of them into account.

III

Torah predicates, in the first place, the need of being God-conscious in all our behavior as individuals and as a People.

It has been said of late in circles which hitherto ignored religion, that a movement like Zionism, aiming to bring about the reawakening of the Jewish spirit, stultifies itself by excluding religion from its scope. The late Hayim Greenberg, in his last address to the World Zionist Congress in July, 1951 had this to say: "This brings us, willingly or not, to the question of religion and religious tradition in Judaism. The tribune from which I speak is not the safest nor the most detached forum for discussing questions of religion. But religion is not something sealed away somewhere in private seclusion, without relation to a people's or to humanity's culture. Religion is itself culture and I am inclined to believe that, potentially, it is indeed the peak of all possible cultural achievement. The archetypal motivation of the Jewish People, its struggles with itself, with the despotism of nature and the pressures of the peoples of the world, sought religious channels, religious implements and religious forms of expression."

It is evident that Hayim Greenberg, and the thousands far less articulate who deplore the religionless character of the majority of our People, do not contemplate the integration of traditional religion into the Zionist movement. Yet, neither he nor anyone else has ever tried to set forth specifically how we should envisage this religion which they now so sorely miss.

By right, the task of answering that question devolves upon the modern rabbinical seminaries and Jewish thinkers. It should be their obligation to collaborate in seeking a solution to this most crucial problem of our future as Jews. The challenge of modern nationalism and socialism to God-centered religion has to be met. A way also has to be found to protect freedom of thought and conscience against the attrition of those who assume that they have a monopoly on religious truth. The problem of achieving a this-worldly type of religion, which should raise the spiritual standards of Jewish life without tampering with the inalienable rights of the individual, is far too complex to be solved by any individual.

Nevertheless, if we are ever to overcome the frustration resulting from speaking in vague generalities, we must make some beginning, and indicate what we should mean by God, and how being God-conscious should make a difference in our lives. Our concern is, of course, with those who can no longer think of God in anthropmorphic terms. If we cannot subscribe to the historicity of the miracles recorded in the Bible, including the theophany on Mount Sinai, *the only way to become God-conscious is to acquire religious literacy. This is a new human requirement which has arisen out of man's recent intellectual progress.*

That progress consists in the discovery of the mechanics of the physical universe and of the human body. Through that discovery man has learned to predict the outcome of physical conditions and to bring many of them under his control. In ancient times, people always associated Godhood with the superhuman aid which they were wont to invoke in order to be helped instead of harmed by whatever in their surroundings possessed power. Religion dominated by that conception of Godhood was magical in character. When, however, men learned to control floods and pestilences, and to achieve soil fertility and personal health by mechanical means, they began to conclude that Godhood was an illusion, and that magical religion was superstition.

It has become evident by this time, however, that unless man give dominance to the drive in himself to rise above his animal nature, he is likely to be destroyed by the achievements of his material progress. His survival depends upon his learning to see the source of that drive as cosmic, or as divine. Conscious reference to, and frequent communion with, that source are essential if man is to be true to the best in himself, and interact with his fellow-men in a spirit of mutual aid and responsibility. Religion in which God is conceived in the foregoing terms is sure to be ethical in character.

IV

That kind of ethical religion, though most conspicuous in the teaching of the Prophets, is by no means confined to Judaism. On the contrary, it has never been wanting in any civilization, except in modern totalitarian civilizations like Nazism and Communism. On the other hand, even in the great historical religions which stress the ethical aspect of Godhood, only ethically sensitized persons have responded to it. For the average person, whether Jew or Gentile, religion has hitherto been important mainly because of its assumed magical character or its function to set in motion physical forces beyond man's control.

The religious issue turns upon the following question: *Can the average Jew be made to realize that: (1) whereas magical religion has been outgrown, ethical religion has become indispensable,* and (2) *the main motivation for Jews to reclaim Eretz Yisrael and to continue as an identifiable group in the Diaspora must derive from ethically oriented Jewish religion and the way it is lived?*

If Zionism is to draw an affirmative response, it has to stress the need for religious literacy. It should place a premium not only on the knowledge of Hebrew but also on the cultural and spiritual duty to know the role that religion has played in the lives of men and societies. One of the main sources of religious literacy should, of course, be our religious literature. A knowledge of the natural history of religion and of the well established facts and generalizations concerning religion in the human sciences, is as indispensable nowadays for a proper orientation to what goes on in man's world, as is a high-school knowledge of the physical sciences to an orientation in the physical world. In the light of the principle of religious literacy, commitment to Torah would mean a renewed study of the entire Jewish past in a spirit of free inquiry. The inquiring spirit must be encouraged from childhood on. There must be no taboos limiting the child's right to question and to receive candid answers to his queries.

One may have an encyclopedic knowledge of literature, philosophy, the arts and the sciences and yet be religiously illiterate. "The psychologist and the social scientist," writes Harry Elmer Barnes, "are far better equipped to handle the religious problem than the most eminent physicist or chemist living, provided the latter has not also acquired a complete command of those aspects of social science which are essential to the intelligent study of religion. . . The pious physicist is a person whose scientific views are on an adult plane, while in the religious field he is intellectually a youth in short pants" (*The Twilight of Christianity*, pp. 31-33 and 357). What is true of physicists and chemists may also be true of archaeologists and philologists. Had Max Nordau, for example, despite his vast knowledge of literature and psychology, not been religiously illiterate, he never could have identified Judaism entirely with religion, or religion exclusively with supernaturalism, nor would he have accepted without examination the "conventional lies" that had been spread by the anti-Semitic scholars concerning the Jewish Scriptures.

Many are the false assumptions concerning religion which misled some of the greatest thinkers. With all their wide knowledge and insight in all other matters, they were totally ignorant as to the facts of religion. They never troubled themselves to study the facts of human behavior as expressed in religion. They simply allowed their prejudices to play upon their imagination. The eighteenth century philosophers, for example, were convinced that religion was a fraud perpetrated by priests, and nineteenth century scientists were likewise certain that it was either an illusion or an opiate. Both were as guilty of wilful ignorance of the facts as the naive fundamentalists who accept tradition blindly.

A proper orientation to religion today requires taking into account its evolution from the proto-conscious stage of society, when many of its magical practices began to be formed, to the progressively conscious stages, when those practices began to take on new meanings as knowledge of reality advanced. It is equally essential to learn to distinguish in religion two distinct strands: one, the magical strand, whose objective is the acquisition of power to satisfy the basic physiological and social needs, and the other, the ethical, whose objective is the realization of the highest latent potentialities in man.

As men begin to master the forces of nature, they do not necessarily abandon their magical practices, even though they give up their magical beliefs. Those magical practices, through having established a common collective consciousness, tend to lose their magical significance and to take on the rationally useful function of cultivating the collective consciousness as a medium of personal religious experience. It then becomes the task of religion to transform the collective consciousness into a means of humanizing the individual and drawing out the best in him. God represents for the collective consciousness the source and goal of its aspirations.

Religious literacy by itself is by no means sufficient, since it is merely knowledge about religion. It presupposes religious experience, whether mystical or pragmatic. Religious experience of the average person, which is mediated and pragmatic, is habituation and training in practices that direct the mind to God as the Power that makes for salvation. But when, as a result of revolutionary changes in men's outlook and mode of living, the chain of religious experience in a people's consciousness is broken, the only way it can be repaired is through religious literacy.

"Only a generation which has been educated through religion, or at least on a religious level, to discriminate between immediate advantage and the lasting issues of life will be capable of accepting the sacrifice which a properly planned democratic order must continually demand from every single group and individual in the interest of the whole" (Karl Mannheim, *Diagnosis of Our Time,* p. 112).

The requirement to achieve a proper orientation to religion is in line of continuity with the oft repeated admonition in Scriptures to strive to "know" God, and with the description of the Millennium as an era when "the earth will be full of knowledge of God." The fact that an understanding of human nature is prerequisite to a knowledge of God seems to be conveyed in the

following scripture: "I am ignorant of what man is, and have no
understanding of what is human, neither have I learned any wisdom. How, then, can I have knowledge of God?" (*Proverbs,*
30:3).

As part of religious literacy, we have to discern in the his-
tories and traditions of all peoples the gradual revelation of divinity,
but most of all in the history and tradition of our own People,
because we are part of that People. That is sufficient reason why
we cannot afford to accept the suggestion of Ben Gurion and
others to treat the entire history of our People after the destruction of the Second Temple and its Rabbinic tradition merely as
a hiatus. Every period of Jewish history is rich in religious experience, provided we discern in it the power of unconquerable faith
in those values that reveal the divine in human life.

Rousseau, in the projected constitution which he wrote for
the Poland of his day, made the point that religious institutions,
festivals and customs were enough to help a people survive the
loss of independence (Hans Kohn, *Ideas of Nationalism,* p. 253).
Elsewhere Rousseau refers to the Jews as an illustration of the
survival power that inheres in adherence to group mores and
rituals (Salo W. Baron, *Modern Nationalism and Religion,* p. 27).

Only when we have come to understand religion as a manifestation of human nature at its best and highest can we experience it as a revelation of divinity, of that Godhood which manifests
itself in a People's will to break through the obstacles blocking it
from the sources of life, the will and courage to undergo that
metamorphosis which is "a dying unto resurrection." Twice in
the past the Jewish People achieved that metamorphosis in its
own being, with the unconsciousness of the chrysalis and butterfly. Now it has to pass through metamorphosis open-eyed and fully
aware of the present critical stage which should serve as a prelude
to its *Vita Nuova.*

V

If *religious* literacy will enable us Jews to become God-conscious, by helping us to identify God as the Power that makes for
salvation, thus rendering Jewish religion primarily ethical in char-

acter, *ethical* literacy will have to be fostered in order to enable us to identify and achieve this-worldly salvation. To be ethically literate is to know "what man is, how he got to be the way he is now, in all the varieties of his being and behavior, and even to recommend procedures which may change both his being and behavior. The facts about human beings, as the anthropologist has unfolded them, have played a very considerable role in the improvement of human relations" (*Cf.* M. F. Ashley Montagu, "Statement on Race," *The Chicago Jewish Forum,* Vol. XI, no. 4). Since that is the case, the human sciences are an indispensable part of an ethical education. One can find much in the various publications of UNESCO, like its *Statement on Race* (1952) and its *The Concept of Race* (1953), that is worthy of being included in the study of Torah.

The time is long past when we can leave the problem of right and wrong to intuition and good will. We have come to realize that, if we are not to depend merely upon tradition, or upon those who speak in its name, to define for us the meaning of right and wrong, we have to be trained, and to train ourselves, to think and act ethically as self- and inner-directed persons. An objective study of what is usually deemed ethical points to the following assumptions: (a) freedom of will and responsibility for our conduct are essential prerequisites to being human; (b) the choice which expresses such freedom is between subhuman resort to violence and coercion and the human resort to principle and persuasion; and (c) every human being, as an end in himself, possesses certain inalienable rights.

The foregoing assumptions derive from the very nature of cosmic reality. Stated in terms of that reality, they may be expressed as follows: That action or attitude is ethical in which a harmonious synthesis is established in man between his inherent drive to be himself (individuation) and the equally inherent drive to interact with his fellows (interaction). The interaction, to be ethical, has to arise from free will on the part of those who thus interact. What is true of the individual is equally true of collectives. They, too, are ethical to the extent that they express their individuality and at the same time interact with other groups.

This polarity in human life is not only ethical; when fully actualized, it constitutes fulfillment or salvation. This polarity, however, is not limited to human life. It is inherent in every element and in every organic group of elements in the universe, thus justifying the assumption that the polarity which constitutes salvation for man transcends man. That is equivalent to saying that God, as the Power that makes for salvation, is cosmic and transcendent, and is not merely immanent in man or society.

In the light of the foregoing, we can discern the full significance of the ethical element in Torah, with its entire context of precepts and teachings relating to the need for being fellow-man-conscious. That need led Rabbi Akiva to state that the main principle of the Torah is: "Thou shalt love they neighbor as thyself," and Ben Azai to say that the main principle of the Torah is implied in the verse: "When God created man he made him in the likeness of God" (Gen. R. XXIV). For only as we behold the divine in our fellow-man, do we know him for what he has essentially in common with us.

Translated into current vocabulary, their statements amount to saying that the main purpose of the Torah is to have everyone treat his fellow-man as a human person. *A human being is a person, insofar as he is potentially self-conscious, rational and purposive.* He would be treated as a "thou" and not as an "it." He should, accordingly, never be treated only as a means, but mainly as an end. Personality is an ever progressive achievement, a growing potentiality made actual through social interaction in family life, education, politics, economics and other human relationships. All these forms of social interaction have to be deliberately aimed towards rendering human beings sufficiently mature to be free and self-directing. How that is to be achieved should be spelled out in life-long study, discussion and guided practice.

Personality, in ourselves and in others, thus assumes the primacy of freedom and justice in our interpersonal and intergroup relations. Freedom means the unhampered functioning of self-hood. Justice means the unhampered functioning of social interaction on the basis of equality, which is the recognition that all human beings have an inalienable right to become fully human.

The incalculable increase in power which men have acquired, due to their material progress, has come too rapidly for them to learn how to distribute that power so that it might augment freedom and justice instead of actually diminishing it. This accounts for the current moral lag.

Modern nationalism and Soviet communism are attempts, actuated for the most part by emotional drives like aggression and hate, to achieve freedom and justice. They have proved to be self-defeating. The totalitarian and authoritarian methods which they have found it necessary to employ violate the sacredness of the human person. If mankind were without self-corrective moral resilience, its doom would, indeed, be inevitable.

It is not too much to expect of our Torah tradition that, with the reconstitution of our Peoplehood and the reclamation of Eretz Yisrael, it be brought sufficiently up to date to enable us Jews to figure henceforth as a society highly endowed with the self-corrective moral resilience of which mankind is so badly in need. In Israel, Jews have the opportunity to develop legislation that would seek to harmonize freedom and justice. "Our Declaration of Independence," said Ambassador Eban, "has its honored place amidst the documents of democratic history, for it inaugurated the life of a free parliamentary society, inspired by Hebrew prophetic tradition as well as by English common law and the robust egalitarian ideals of the American and French revolutions" (*Israel Digest,* May 17, 1954). None but a narrow-minded fanatic could object to including such a Declaration of Independence in the *corpus* of Torah teaching.

What the late Professor Louis Ginzberg wrote about the need of legislation when Judea achieved independence under Hasmonean rule, applies with redoubled force to our day: "The development of commerce and trade under the Hasmonean rulers peremptorily called for the building up of a code of civil law. The few rules found in Scriptures bearing on this branch of law were not sufficient and could not be made so, not even by the most subtle reasoning or cleverest interpretation. The time was certainly ripe for legislation. Every student of the history of jurisprudence knows that great as are the possibilities of interpretation and commentation, an old code has limits which cannot be stretched. When the breaking-point is reached legislation comes to the rescue, abrogating obsolete laws and adding new ones which conform to the demands of the age" ("Introduction," *A Commentary on the Palestinian Talmud,* N. Y., Jewish Theological Seminary, 1941, p. XIV).

That by no means obviates the need of fostering in Israel both studies and experiments in the *ethical* aspect of human relations. Ethics is generally distinguished from law, in that it cannot depend on the use of sanctions; it calls for a sensitive and enlightened conscience. This distinction, however, not only is misleading but can, and often does, lead to harmful consequences. It is one of those dichotomies on which the human mind falls back, when it finds itself unable to grasp the polarity of a situation. Actually human law that is worthy of the name should be the controlled embodiment of ethical principle, and all ethical principles should find controlled embodiment in law.

An outstanding illustration of what Zionism has been able to achieve in that regard is the *Histadrut* in Israel. Jews the world over should not merely be proud of the great ethical achievement of *Histadrut,* but should study, understand and as far as possible incorporate in their own communal life some of the high ethical standards which that organization has demonstrated as feasible in human society. The basic principle of *Histadrut* is stated in the opening paragraph of its constitution: "The Histadrut unites all workers who subsist on earning of their own work, and who do not exploit the labor of others, in order to provide for all communal, economic and cultural matters relating to the working class in Palestine, with a view to the establishment of a Jewish laboring community in this country" (Samuel Kurland, *Cooperative Palestine,* New York, 1947, p. 265). The *Histadrut* is probably the largest organization in the world in which human dignity, human equality and the equal dignity of all labor are not merely utopian ideals, but hard, matter of fact, literal realities which govern the lives of hundreds of thousands of men, women and children. This improvement of the workers' lot and status has been achieved without resort to the totalitarian, brutal and dehumanizing methods of Marxist communism.

It is mainly in the Diaspora that the Torah requirement of being fellow-man-conscious will have to be met through the replenishment of Jewish ethics. The issue between the self-directed and free personality, on the one hand, and the authority- and tradition-directed personality, on the other hand, was never drawn in the past as sharply as it is today. Never was the human person in such danger of being reduced to a cog in some vast human machine, be it nation, class, managerial, labor or professional group, as he is today.

"Let us be on our guard," said Nahum Goldmann recently, "in a common front with all who adhere to the idea of human freedom, of individual liberty and intellectual tolerance. It is our destiny—it should ever be our willing obligation—to be everywhere in the forefront for these ideas, even when these ideas are unfashionable or unpopular. These ideas alone can create the climate in which we can live, and so long as they are threatened anywhere in the world, our position will remain unsafe" (*The Status of Jewry,* the World Jewish Congress). *Since the climate of opinion which prevails in the world can no longer be the one which our tradition generated, let us at least help to make it one which is so akin to the ethical spirit of our tradition as to enable us to maintain our sense of individuality and continuity with the People of the Bible and the Talmud.*

VI

A spiritual need of the modern Jew is that of being religiously world-conscious. That is the need of sanctifying mundane interests by using them as means to individual and collective salvation. Only the Torah as a way of life, creatively expanded to meet the demands of modern living, can cope with that need.

1. The fundamental error of the traditional assumption concerning human nature was that, since men tended to succumb to worldly temptation, they should as far as possible withdraw from

the world and devote themselves to the contemplation of God and communion with Him. Likewise, they should abstain from too much intercourse with their fellow-men, and seek their own salvation in solitude. This gave rise to asceticism.

The modern reaction against other-worldliness is a form of this-worldliness, known as secularism. It centers all its hopes for the future of humanity upon man's ability to manipulate the forces of nature for the production of all kinds of goods and gadgets to feed his unlimited appetite for pleasure and power. The attainment of this goal calls for collectivization of human energy and brain power. Collectivization, whether it be in the interests of capital or labor, whether it be for the purpose of marketing products or obtaining raw material, or whether it take on political or economic form, gives rise to irreconcilable conflicts that threaten the survival of mankind. This is the inevitable outcome of the secularism which has progressively been making man a slave of this world.

A third alternative to withdrawal from the world and being mastered by it is to master the world. That alternative is stated in the teaching of the Torah concerning man's place in creation. According to that teaching, God has put everything under man's feet, and it is man's prerogative to master the world (*Cf*. Genesis 1:28, Isaiah, 45:18, Psalm 8:7). This contrasts with the exhortation "to keep oneself unspotted from the world" (James 1:27) which deprecates material interests as inherently impure, as well as with the advice of the secularists that we should submit to the world. In keeping with that prerogative, the strengthening of man's power over the forces of nature is not to be viewed as an attempt to do away with dependence upon God, but rather as bringing to fruition the divine potentialities latent in human intelligence.

This God-conscious view of man's power should imbue man with a high sense of responsibility for the way he uses it. *Mankind would have been spared its present dread anxieties, had the rapid growth in the ability to manipulate atomic energy been accompanied by a similar growth in the responsibility for the use of that energy.*

Likewise, the alternative to this-worldliness expressed in "a hypertrophy of collectivization" would not have to be an other-worldliness which only a select few can find in monasteries and the rest in occasional retreats. Being fellow-man-conscious in the spirit of the numerous Torah precepts which are applications of the one to love our fellow-man (Lev. 19:18) would impel us to devise ways and means of retaining the dignity and sacredness of the human person in ourselves and in our neighbors.

2. The other legitimate way of being world-conscious or mastering the world, is to cultivate the mundane interests and tastes that are expressed in the fine arts. Aesthetic culture must henceforth occupy a place in the life of the spirit. In the other-worldly thought-universe which prevailed in the pre-modern centuries no special significance was attached to aesthetic culture *per se*. It was important only insofar as it was a means to evoke and express the God-consciousness. All literature, reflection and art were God-centered. Accordingly, in the past, Torah could mean to Jews only those elements of Jewish culture which were God-centered, or only to the extent that they were God-centered.

For Torah to continue to function vitally in the life of the Jewish People, it has to stimulate Jewish creativity in literature, in poetry and in the fine arts. "One does wrong," writes Thomas Mann, in *Dr. Faustus,* "to see in aesthetics a separate and narrow field of the humane." While it is important for the various aspects of Jewish culture to be cultivated as ends in themselves and for for their own sake, they should also be means of expressing the *creative* spirit of the Jewish People. In that way they will avert the possibility of becoming rootless and sterile. How far Jewish cultural creativity will consciously, or unconsciously, relate itself to, and draw upon, the concrete Jewish tradition will depend upon the extent to which that tradition will have been spelled out into specific applications of the three fundamental Torah-conceptions of being God-conscious, fellow-man-conscious, and world-conscious.

In order that Jewish cultural development be an integral part of Torah, it has to be sustained by the Hebrew language as the chief medium of Jewish self-expression. Hebrew is indispensable

as a means of giving the Jew, wherever he resides, a feeling of
continuity with the Jewish past and of unity with the entire Jewish
People, whose very reality often escapes the Jews of the Diaspora.

The Hebrew language· is actually identified in our tradition
with Torah, as is evident from the numerous statements concerning it throughout Rabbinic literature. "In the name of R. Meir
was it taught that he who lives permanently in Eretz Yisrael . . .
and converses in the Holy Tongue (Hebrew) is certain to have a
share in the world to come" (*J. Shab.* III, *Cf. Sifre on Deut.*
11:19). Maimonides accounts speaking in Hebrew as one of the
most important *mitzvot* of the Torah (*Cf.* Commentary on Avot
II, 1). On the other hand, it was none other than a free-thinker
like Nordau who wrote: "Never was Hebrew more holy than when
it aided in the preparation of the Jewish People for the great task
which its historic evolution begins to unveil before our eyes" (Nordau's Preface to *Paradoksim,* translated by Reuben Brainin, Warsaw, Epstein, 1920, pp. I-IV, May 8, 1900).

VII

The foregoing discussion of how the Torah is to be made
responsive to man's contemporary higher needs is intended mainly
for Diaspora Jewry, as a means of fostering their Jewish life and
experiencing the indispensability of Eretz Yisrael as a spiritual
motherland. If we took into account the needs of the Jewish community in Israel, which is to serve the core of world Jewry, we
would have to give first place to the more immediate and pressing
problem of expanding the Torah to include the manifold tasks
and duties that have arisen concerning political existence as a
modern independent state, tasks and duties that have never been
contemplated in traditional Jewish law.

At this point we have to refer again to the yeoman service
rendered by Yeshaia Leibovitz, of the Hebrew University, in posing
the problem presented by the limited scope of traditional Jewish
law. "The 'regime of the Torah' as expressed in the Halakha is a
way of life for a man who does not include in the plans and pros-
pects of his life the functions and duties of a responsible citizen of
a state; it is a regime of a community which can dispense with

problems of defense, of internal and external security, of foreign affairs and diplomatic relations, of the keeping of an army and a police and an administrative apparatus, of the decision on war and peace, of production for the supply of its own needs, even of a judiciary which functions not by voluntary consent of the parties but by compulsion" ("Religion and State," *The Jerusalem Post,* September 9, 1952).

What is happening in Israel as a result of its Jews' failing to expand the Torah in keeping with the dimensions of contemporary needs is summed up in the following: "The lack of a real program for a socio-political regime according to the Torah, combined with organized activities on the political stage for 'religious demands' turns the great struggle for the Torah into clerical politics and tactics; there is no struggle for a definite, comprehensive and all-embracing vision of a special way of life of a people, but only petty encroachments on the freedom of private life" (*Ibid.*).

To achieve, however, an "all-embracing vision of a special way of life of a people," much more is needed than suggested by Yeshaia Leibovitz in any of his published writings. It is true that he has come to realize that traditional Judaism is in need of reconstruction. But his notion of reconstruction is like that of one who, when he finds that the three-story dwelling in which he has been living has become inadequate, proceeds to build three more stories on top of it without examining the foundation to see whether it could bear the additional weight of the new building. To change the analogy, nothing less than a Copernican revolution in our entire outlook leading to our becoming God-conscious, fellow-man-conscious and world-conscious, in terms of universal wisdom, will move both Israeli and Diaspora Jews to undertake the enlargement of Torah as a means of rendering the Jewish People a highly civilized and humane factor for universal freedom, justice and brotherhood.

In sum: the present crisis in the Zionist movement is but a phase of the crisis in Judaism. The only way to overcome the crisis in Zionism is to deal with the conditions responsible for the crisis in Judaism. In other words, Jewish loyalty has to be motivated anew for all Jews throughout the world. They have to be made to feel that Jewish life is intrinsically worth while and indispensable to their self-fulfillment or salvation. That feeling can derive only from the reconstitution of the Jewish People, the reclamation of Eretz Yisrael and the creative expansion of Torah.

Zionism can emerge from its present crisis strengthened by the experience of challenge and danger. It can become the custodian of the Jewish future. It can lead to the fulfillment of the prophecy that "from Zion shall go forth Torah." But before the Torah can go forth from Zion, it will have to enter into Zionism.

BIBLIOGRAPHY

ERICH FROMM, *Escape from Freedom*, N. Y. ,1941.

——. *Man for Himself*, N. Y., 1947.

MORDECAI M. KAPLAN, "Torah," Part Six in *Judaism as a Civilization*, N. Y. 1934.

——. "The Next Stage in Jewish Religion" and "Toward a New Pattern for Jewish Life," in *The Future of the American Jew*, N. Y., 1947.

——. *The Meaning of God in Modern Jewish Religion*, N. Y., 1937.

E. G. LEE, *Mass Man and Religion*, N. Y., (no date).

KARL MANNHEIM, *The Diagnosis of Our Time*, N. Y., 1944.

E. DUDLEY WARD (Ed.), *Goals of Economic Life*, N. Y., 1953.

CHAPTER VII

Why A Greater Zionism?

THE PRESENT CONDITION OF ZIONISM may be compared to that of the Negro Joe in *Showboat,* where he sings "Ol' Man River" and speaks of himself as "being tired o'livin' and afeard o'-dyin'." A movement that is as old biologically as it is chronologically, is on the way out. That is the predicament in which the Zionist Movement finds itself at the present time. The proportion of its younger to its elder statesmen is far too small for the good of the movement. To live is to renew oneself. So far, American Zionism, like American Judaism, can hardly be said to be showing sings of renewing itself, or even of possessing the power to renew itself. A son of an American Zionist is more of an American than his father, probably more cultured generally, and more efficient in business or the professions than his father, but he is certainly less of a Jew and less of a Zionist than his father.

The primary requisite for the renewal of Zionism is to counteract the *psychological* effect of the various efforts in which American Jews engage to enable the State of Israel to weather its political storms. Strangely enough, the psychological effect of those efforts is to produce a distorted idea of Zionism. In the minds of many Jews and most non-Jews, Zionism has come to be thought of mainly as a refugee movement which has given rise to an Arab refugee problem. Instead of being considered as a long range process of a people trying to transform itself, Zionism has come to be dealt with as an emergency affair, with reaction to immediate events as the sole form of action. Before proceeding to discuss what has

to be done to counteract the dangerous misconception of
Zionism as essentially a refugee movement, let us try to recall
what was the main intent of its founders and architects.

CLASSICAL ZIONISM

The truth is that classical Zionism is nothing less than a
desperate effort on the part of the Jewish people to rise out
of the valley of dead bones, to become, in the words of Herzl,
"once again the subject of history and not only its object," to
give the lie to pseudo-philosophers who maintain that the Jewish People is a fossil, and to confound the large host of its
enemies who charge it with being nothing but an international
intruder and a trouble maker. To a Rabbi Kalisher, to an
Ahad Haam, to a Herzl, and to a Gordon, to a Berl Katzenel-
son, and to a Ben-Gurion, Zionism spells nothing less than the
resurrection of the Jewish People. To those of us to whom the
Jewish People is fundamentally the bearer of Judaism as a religious civilization, Zionism is Judaism, bursting its cerements
and stepping out of its mummified condition. To all Jews
who have a deep concern for the future of the Jewish People,
and its place in the comity of nations, classical Zionism is
Messiah in modern dress, and not in rags in which, according
to a Rabbinic legend, he sat at the gate of Rome, bandaging
his wounds. Zionism is the Messiah not riding on a donkey
but commuting in a jet plane.

Wherein may Zionism be regarded as Messiah?

In the first place, its aim is to change the Jews from a
ghost people, which they have been ever since they were freed
from their civil disabilities, into a living world community.
In a set of volumes called *The Jews—Their Culture and Religion,* edited by Dr. Finkelstein, the Chancellor of The Jewish Theological Seminary of America, an entire chapter is
devoted to the question—"Who are the Jews?" written by no
less an authority than the noted Professor of Anthropology
Melville J. Herskovits. His conclusion is that no definition
in terms of race or culture or belief can fit the Jews as a
group. "Yet," he says, "the Jews do represent a historic con-

tinuum and have survived as an identifiable, yet constantly shifting series of groups. Is there," he adds, "any least common denominator other than the designation Jew?" It is seriously to be questioned. A word can mean many things to many people; and no word, one may almost conclude, means more things to more people than does the word "Jew." That this statement is not mere academic palaver, but represents a very serious condition in the life of the Jewish People, is evidenced by the fact that in Israel the question—"who is a Jew?"—has become a political football between the religionists and the secularists. No less a serious symptom of the amorphous ghost-like character of the Jewish People is the order issued by the Minister of Education in Israel that the elementary and secondary schools introduce the teaching of a subject known as "Jewish Consciousness."

Classical or genuine Zionism is messianic in that it attempts not only to put an end to the seeming unreality of the Jewish People, but to save whatever reality the Jewish People still possesses from being an unclassifiable entity, a kind of social absurdity or misfit. That the Jewish People should be a problem in definition was inconceivable before the beginning of the nineteenth century. The general configuration of mankind was then such that the Jews could regard themselves as a nation in exile hoping to be restored to its homeland, and could be regarded as such by the rest of the world. That configuration no longer exists in modern life. Mankind is divided into sovereign state-nations, each of which is identified with a specific territory. The only form of large-scale societies which are independent of territorial boundaries are world religious communities like Christendom and Islam. The Jewish People, or House of Israel, cannot be considered either a sovereign nation or a landless religious body. With the virtual ending of Jewish segregation, the status of the Jews has become an enigma. Though that enigma is regarded as having been solved for the Jews who settled in Israel, it has remained unsolved for the Jewish People as a whole.

JEWISH STATUS

The Jews themselves are of a divided mind with regard to the status of those of their numbers who do not expect to migrate to Israel. Some consider themselves, and are considered by their fellow-Jews, as being in exile. That places them in a far more abnormal condition than Jews were ever in during the past. When an influential Zionist who vociferously denies the possibility of a Jewish future in the Diaspora is asked why he does not migrate to Israel, his answer is that he knows that he lives in sin. Apparently living in sin agrees with him. Other Jews, who refuse to accept the status of exile for what they believe to be their permanent condition in the Diaspora, for a time played with the idea of considering themselves as members of a trans-national religious community. They had renounced all hope for and claim to Eretz Yisrael. Events have proved them to be out of keeping with the realities of the Jewish situation. So far no alternative classification, status, or category into which all who are known as Jews might be placed, has been arrived at. We are thus a people in search of a definition. In short we don't really know who and what we are. How long can a people retain its sanity under that condition?

If Zionism is to be true to its messianic purpose, it cannot afford to regard the establishment of the State of Israel as having solved the troublesome problem of "Who is a Jew, and what is the Jewish People?" As a consequence the Jews who do not migrate to Israel are lacking a recognized group to give them a personal status and security. Unless that problem be solved, the very notion of transmitting a Jewish heritage from one generation to another as a special obligation of Jewish parents to their children is meaningless, since the purpose of any social heritage is to maintain the continuity of a group or society that has a name, a purpose and a will to live. Where one sees no visible evidence of such a group or society, one feels alienated. If one is young, one is liable to become a member of the spiritually "shook-up" youth. Before the establishment of the State of Israel, this messianic task of solving the enigma of "where is the Jewish People?" could not have been felt as imperatively and as urgently as we feel it now.

Secondly, events beyond all human control did unquestionably compel the Zionist movement to concentrate all its energies upon the creation of a sovereign state for the Jewish People. The growing hostility of the European nations towards the Jews, which culminated in the extermination of more than one-third of the Jewish People, while the rest of the world refused to intervene, had accentuated the homelessness of European Jews to a degree which made their condition unbearable. They needed a homeland where they could experience some sense of security. Home is said to be the place where, when you have to go there, they have to let you in. So urgent was that need felt by Leon Pinsker and Theodor Herzl, the fathers of the Zionist Movement, that they were willing to accept any territory whatever, not necessarily Eretz Yisrael, which Jews might make into a home. But those in whom the basic drive to Zion had been motivated by the messianic purpose of salvaging the entire Jewish People from disintegration, could not associate the feeling of home with any land other than Eretz Yisrael. They turned down the offer of Uganda, even as a temporary stopping place on the way to Eretz Yisrael. Now that the State of Israel has at last become a reality, the problem is how to keep it from becoming destroyed by the Arab nations which outnumber the Jews of Israel as twenty to one. Whatever else Zionism must aim for, this objective is the first order of priority.

ZIONISM'S MESSIANIC CHARACTER

A third aspect of the messianic character of Zionism, one for which Zionism is mainly deserving of the adjective "messianic" has been the expectation of activating anew the spiritual, idealistic or religious purpose to which the Jewish People has always considered itself dedicated or covenanted. To Kalisher it meant resuming the religious life in Eretz Yisrael

at the point at which it had been cut off when it was driven
away from its homeland. To Ahad Haam, Zionism meant the
planning of a social order which would be in keeping with
the exhortations of the great prophets. To A. D. Gordon the
return of the Jews to Eretz Yisrael made sense only if they
undertook to establish there an economic order free from
parisitism and evolve into what he called a human people,
through a return to nature and the repudiation of all social
values based on power of man over man.

Certainly Zionism is far from being a finished business. It
could hardly be regarded as messianic, if it were to content
itself with having established a State, even were the future of
that state guaranteed. Such a denouement to a three thousand
year struggle of a people, that has in part succeeded in giving
meaning to human life and history, would dispel that very
meaning. From the viewpoint of the future of the Jewish
People, almost as important as having called into being the
State of Israel, is for Zionism to call into being the social instrument that would arrive at a new status or classification for
the Jewish People as a trans-national people with its core in
Eretz Yisrael. That new status or classification must embrace a
purpose or meaning to Jewish life that is of universal import
because of its idealistic, cosmic, spiritual or religious character.
Only such a purpose or meaning would give direction to the
life of the Jewish People and help the rest of the world to
understand it for what it actually is, thereby removing once
and for all, the inexcusable, as well as excusable, reasons for
their misapprehension and blind prejudices.

THE MODERNITY OF ZIONISM

What is there to Zionism that makes of it Messiah in
modern dress? What is there modern about it? In the first
place, it urges the Jews to unlearn the long-standing inveter-
ate habit of waiting passively for redemption, to renounce the
traditional taboo against forcing prematurely the hoped for
redemption. In pre-modern times that taboo saved the Jews
from coming into a head-on collision with overwhelming

forces which would have annihilated them. But that taboo has not only outlived its function; it has become a source of danger. With it must go its attendant belief that the future redemption would be like what tradition had taught concerning the redemption of our early ancestors from Egypt and their conquest of Canaan. According to tradition, nature would stop in its course; the sun and the moon would be outdone by the resplendent light of God; the most cruel beasts would be tamed, and the whole earth would be full of the knowledge of the Lord as the waters covered the sea. Instead, Zionism has been reminding us Jews that Divinity will not redeem us, unless we take the initiative in the effort to redeem ourselves. We cannot afford to ignore the lesson that mankind has been learning the last five hundred years concerning the ways of God with man. The essence of that lesson is that if man is to become fully human, he has to reckon with, and avail himself of, the limitations and opportunities of the natural order both in the physical world and in human society. That is the lesson which Zionism has been trying to teach our people for the last three-quarters of a century. That is one aspect of Zionism which makes of it a Messiah in modern dress.

Secondly, the inference to be drawn from that new lesson concerning God's way with man is that the redemption which we must initiate must be compatible with the political and spiritual realities of contemporary society.

At present the State of Israel is in a precarious condition. Internationally, it is resting, as it were, on a volcano which may erupt at any moment. With the East and the West courting the Arab nations, which have only one aim in common—that of destroying the State of Israel, Zionists cannot afford to rest on the laurels of what they have already achieved. No matter how difficult it is to win the goodwill of the West, without arousing the bitter hostility of the East, they must not give up trying. This is where the modern aspect of Zionism must assert itself. Instead of hoping that somehow, by some kind of supernatural miracle, the fires which threaten to erupt from the volcano will be extinguished and the State of Israel will be saved, Zionism should bring the case of the Jewish People before the court of world opinion in such a way as to have mankind realize that to allow the State of Israel to be destroyed is to be guilty of genocide and ethnocide.

The statement of the case for the Jewish People must so present the cause of Jewish survival as to win the goodwill of the nations of the world. It should spell out clearly to what extent the highest interests of civilization would be served by permitting the Jews in the Diaspora to retain their Jewish individuality, without thereby preventing their political and cultural integration into the various nations of which they are a part.

Even more specifically and immediately, Zionism should make it its objective to find a solution for the Arab refugee problem which is at present the greatest threat that hangs over the State of Israel. *As Zionists, we must realize that whatever threatens the State of Israel is a threat to the life of the Jewish People throughout the world.* Zionists must therefore leave no stone unturned in their efforts to court public opinion and win the goodwill of the nations for the State of Israel.

UNREALISTIC EXPECTATIONS

Let us turn to another aspect of the messianic character of Zionism. We must remember that, except for the occasional mass massacres perpetrated against our Jewish People, the most tragic experience which it has undergone has been the one of being disillusioned every time a would-be redeemer or Messiah turned out to be pseudo-Messiah. There were at least eight such so-called false Messiahs. I say "so-called," because actually they were neither impostors nor hypocrites. They were merely self-deluded. They had mistaken notions concerning God's way with man. They believed implicitly in the traditional conception of miracle Messiahs, and they were sincerely convinced that they themselves were endowed with supernatural powers. We must not forget that even a Messiah in modern dress, though not subject to the kind of mistaken thinking of the self-deluded Messiahs, might easily delude himself by trusting his own wishful thinking and imagining it to be the will of God. For that reason, it devolves upon the Zionist movement to prove that it is on its guard against any kind of wishful thinking or self-delusion. It should not keep on repeating cliches which time has shown to be erroneous or outlived. It should always be self-corrective and experimental. It should not allow commitment to its own past to be crippling. It should be ready to admit having made mistakes, and be ever ready to bring its purposes and plans into line with what the realities of the situation demand.

Zionism should recognize and repudiate expectations which have turned out to be unrealistic. To mention just a few: In the first place, the creation of a Jewish State was expected to bring about an end to anti-Semitism. "If we only begin to carry out our plans, anti-Semitism would stop at once and forever," Herzl wrote in *The Jewish State*. Despite his clairvoyance with regard to the growing tendency to make the European continent *Judenrein*, he had not the least concept that bitter Jew -hatred might develop in the Arabic world as a result of the Jews' return to Eretz Yisrael, and that the repercussion of that hatred might reactivate the anti-Semitism after it had gone underground in Christendom. We must remember that anti-Semitism manages to break out even in countries where there are no Jews. Certainly the establishment of the State of Israel has not prevented American hoodlums from bombarding synagogues. Secondly, the Zionist movement, being modern in spirit, necessarily expected at the very start to avail itself of whatever new experiences had been acquired in the arts of government and socio-economic relations by the most advanced nations. However, the founders failed to forsee that this tutelage under the secularized Western civilization might bring about on the part of the Jews in Eretz Yisrael such a complete break with the Jewish past and with the rest of contemporaneous world Jewry as to necessitate the issuance of a special order by the Ministry of Education that the schools should introduce into their

curricula the teaching of "Jewish Consciousness." There is
more to the irony of teaching of Jewish consciousness in Israel's schools than I can spell out at the present time. What
it shows is that, except for the Mizrahists or a thinker like
A. D. Gordon, the founding fathers of Zionism failed to have
the least understanding of the fact that a completely secularized Jewish consciousness was as absurd as the square root of
a minus quantity or that two plus two equals five.

Another serious mistake made by the founders of the
Zionist movement was the assumption that the very atmosphere
of Eretz Yisrael would transform the Jews there into the
avant garde of the Jewish People throughout the world. Ahad
Haam was convinced that the effect of a thriving Jewish life
in Eretz Yisrael would be to bring about a spiritual renaissance among Jews everywhere else. What is actually happening, however, is much more in keeping with what the late
Klatzkin foretold and what Arthur Koestler and Isaiah Berlin
maintain at present, namely that the very existence of a territory in which Jews can feel at home, is bound to give rise
to the assumption, on the part of Jews in the Diaspora, that
they no longer have the moral responsibility of keeping the
Jewish People alive through their refusal to become assimilated with the rest of the world. They need have no further
compunctions about becoming full-fledged *Goyim*. Unfortunately, Jewish life in the Diaspora is certain to take the direction envisaged by the Koestlers and not the .direction envisaged by Ahad Haam, unless Zionism undoes its most serious
blunder. That is the blunder of retaining the traditional belief that the ultimate destiny of the Jewish People is to be
completely ingathered within the boundaries of Eretz Yisrael.
Though included within that conception of Jewish destiny was
the assumption that the Jewish People would wield a world-
wide spiritual influence, such influence would come about
through the journeying of the nations "to the mount of the
House of the Lord in Jerusalem," and not through the dispersion of the Jews among the nations. The entire Jewish

tradition uniformly considers dispersion synonymous with exile. However, that could not possibly be the reason classic Zionism has operated with this traditional conception of Diaspora or dispersion. Since classical Zionism did not hesitate to break with the long Jewish tradition concerning the personal Messiah and the need for waiting passively for his coming, it might as well have broken with the tradition concerning the synonymity of Jewish dispersion with Jewish exile. In the matter of Diaspora Judaism, I believe in "the power of positive thinking."

THE SECURITY OF THE STATE

The main reason that at the moment outstanding Zionists hold on to the traditional conception of Jewish redemption as requiring the concentration of all Jews within Eretz Yisrael is that the security of the State of Israel calls for as large a Jewish population as it can possibly hold. Do they not realize, however, that telling the Jews in the Diaspora that their children will be assimilated will not frighten them into migrating to Israel? The original reason for classical Zionism's negation of the Diaspora had nothing to do with the security of the state. Classical Zionism wished to conform to the trend in a modern type of nationalism. In contrast with pre-modern nationalism, which was based for the most part on a common kinship and a common religion, modern nationalism tends to dissolve the diversities of kinship, religion, language and culture and to replace them by a solidarity based upon common political and economic interests which arise from territorial proximity. Were Zionism, however, to accept this present trend in modern nationalism as inevitable for the Jewish People as well, and therefore resign itself to the gradual elimination of the Jewish People from bodies of other nations, the destiny of world Jewry would shrink to that of a small Levantine nation that would have as little influence on world civilization as any of the other countries in the Middle East. That would indeed spell "finis" once and for all to the historic Jewish People of the book. That would be the end of

the House of Israel which has done more for the shaping of
the spiritual history than any other people of mankind. If
that is the price Zionists are willing to pay for what they believe to be the best interests of the State of Israel, then there
is nothing further to be said.

If, however, Zionists are unwilling to renounce the age-
long dream of the Jewish People that it might play a leading
role in the moral and spiritual progress of mankind, then they
have to call into being a Jewish world assembly that would
devise a new social pattern for the Jewish People whereby
its dispersion would not mean exile, but the opportunity to
have its spiritual and moral influence radiate throughout the
world. That cannot be achieved by any of the Zionist regional
organizations nor even by the World Zionist Organization.
The creation of such a world assembly, a modern Sanhedrin—
not of the Napoleonic type but a body representative of the
entire House of Israel—should henceforth be as much the specific goal of the World Zionist Organization as was before
1948 the creation of the State of Israel. That Jewish World
Assembly would study and translate into action the possibilities that inhere in the common historic kinship of all Jews, in
their common tradition and in their common religion, to weld
into one solidarity or community all who call themselves Jews
and wish to be so recognized. That assembly would have to
do more than merely adopt the traditional or conventional
ideas which have been associated with those three factors that
make for unity. It would have to infuse in the historic kinship,
the common tradition, and the common religion of Jews a
spirit of dynamism or evolution whereby they would become
relevant to and co-extensive with the contemporary climate of
thought and aspiration. In other words, such an assembly
would have to seek ways and means of adapting traditional
ideas and ideals of the Jewish People to what experience has
proven to be true and good instead of the reverse.

WORLD JEWISH ASSEMBLY

It is evident that the greatest obstacle that will have to be
hurdled by such a Jewish World Assembly is the existence of

irreconcilable attitudes among Jews toward religion. After having associated religion from its very inception with supernaturalism, it will undoubtedly not be easy to get Jews to realize that the world outlook and way of life of an A. D. Gordon, though devoid of supernaturalism are as authentically religious as those of a Rav Kook. Both traditionalists and secularists will have to learn to stretch the meaning of religion so that it might include a humanist or secularist version of life.

Many are the dilemmas which confront the Jewish People at present, but none is in such urgent need of being resolved as that of the growing demoralization of a Diaspora Jewry which classical Zionism has consigned to ultimate dissolution. That decree of classical Zionism must be annulled.

RELIGION—A UNIFYING BOND

If we Zionists are determined not only to rescue Jews from persecution and misery, but also to redeem the Jewish People from the danger of disintegration and absorption by the nations of the world, then we must educate every Jewish man, woman and child to transcend the petty and divisive semantic differences as to the meaning of the term religion. We must get them to understand by Jewish religion whatever makes of the consciousness of Jewish Peoplehood a motivating influence for moral character and responsibility which is the revelation of God in the human spirit. This is only one of a thousand ways of defining Jewish religion whereby it should be possible to have all Jews see in religion—however they conceive it—the main unifying bond among all Jews, both in and outside Israel. Such a unifying bond would enable the rest of the world to understand why we Jews wish to assume as a permanent pattern the kind of religious ethnic unity which would enable us to go on living and functioning as a trans-national religious world-fellowship, with its indispensable life-giving center in the Jewish community of the State of Israel.

At present, no doubt, such an achievement seems as remote from possibility, as the establishment of a sovereign state did in the days of Herzl. But what he said then, also holds good now:

"If you will it, it will not remain mere fantasy."

A Proposed Platform For The Greater Zionism

The following is part of a report submitted on behalf of The Commission on Zionist Ideology for action by the ZOA at its convention in Miami Beach October 23-26, 1958:

ZIONISM SHOULD PURSUE the following aims:

1. It should promulgate and translate into action the supreme importance of the centrality of the State of Israel to the survival and spiritual enhancement of the Jewish People throughout the world.

2. It should help to bring about the reaffirmation and reconstitution of world Jewry as a religio-ethnic, transnational People, united by a common history and a common spiritual destiny.

3. It should develop in the Diaspora, to the maximum degree, the creative potentialities of Jewish life, culture and religion.

4. It should foster in the Jewish Community in Israel and in all Jewish communities in the Diaspora a sense of partnership and mutual responsibility in the common endeavor to have the Jewish People throughout the world figure as an indispensable factor in the civilization of mankind.

* * *

With the foregoing aims in view, Zionism should engage in the following activities:

1. It should reassert the historic right of the Jewish People to the Land of Israel as its spiritual homeland, and endeavor to win the full recognition of such rights by the world community of nations.

2. It should also strive to win the goodwill of the Arab nations toward the State of Israel.

3. It should promote Aliyah (migration) to Israel for such various purposes as volunteer professional service, student and teacher interchange and cultural exploration, as well as permanent settlement.

4. It should mobilize the necessary material and spiritual resources for the security and welfare of Israel.

5. It should help to develop the State of Israel as a democratic commonwealth in which there will be the fullest freedom of expression and equality of opportunity in all religious, cultural and socio-economic spheres of life.

6. It should stimulate the existing institutions of elementary, secondary and higher Jewish learning to further an intensive Jewish education of young and old and foster a love for the Hebrew language and literature.

7. It should call upon all communal agencies in the Diaspora such as congregational unions, philanthropic federations, welfare funds, community councils and fraternal orders, to reorganize the structure of Jewish community life and to redirect its spirit, so that it reflect the status and role of the Jews as a world People.

8. It should, in recognition of cultural values as an essential element in a civilization, encourage the fullest possible expression in the Diaspora of Jewish cultural values through literature and the arts.

9. It should urge the World Zionist Organization to call into being a World Jewish Conference for the following purposes:

a) To clarify the status of the Jews as a religio-ethnic transnational People.

b) To define the place of the Jewish People among the peoples of the world and

c) To indicate how Judaism can be compatible, first, with unity in diversity, and continuity in change; secondly, with full participation in the life of the peoples among whom the Jews live; and third, with the inevitable difference in scope and intensity between Jewish life in Israel and Jewish life in the Diaspora.

GENERAL BIBLIOGRAPHY

Books

RUTH NANDA ANSHEN, *Freedom*,. N. Y., 1940.

JOHN BAILLIE, *Invitation to Pilgrimage*, N. Y., 1942.

HENRY STEEL COMMAGER, *The American Mind*, New Haven, 1950.

W. A. DUNNING, *A History of Political Ideas*, N. Y., 1920.

NAHUM N. GLATZER, *Franz Rosenzweig*, Phila., 1953.

D. W. HARDING, *Social Psychology and Individual Values*, London, 1953.

HANS KOHN, *The Idea of Nationalism*, N. Y., 1944.

SAMUEL KURLAND, *Cooperative Palestine*, N. Y., 1947.

HARRY ORLINSKY, *Ancient Israel*, N. Y., 1954.

DAVID PHILIPSON, *The Reform Movement in Judaism*, N. Y., 1931.

ELIEZER RIEGER, *Hahinukh Haivri B'Eretz Yisrael*, Jerusalem, 1939.

MARION SIMMS, *The Bible in America*, N. Y., 1936.

Articles

S. H. BERGMANN, "Israel and the Diaspora," *Forum*, 1953.

PHILIP BERNSTEIN, "New Year Message," *Opinion*, Sept.-Oct., 1954.

DANIEL J. BOORSTIN, "Our Unspoken National Faith," *Commentary*, April, 1953.

HORACE L. FRIESS, "A Unity of Spirit," *The Standard*, May-June, 1954.

NAHUM GOLDMANN, "Herzl and the Jewish State," *Jewish Frontier*, Sept., 1954.

SIMON HALKIN, "Zionism and the State of Israel," *Forum*, 1953.

HORACE M. KALLEN, "Whither Israel?", *Menorah Journal*, Vol. 39, No. 2.

M. F. ASHLEY MONTAGU, "Statement on Race," *Chicago Jewish Forum*, Vol. XI, No. 4.

JACOB J. WEINSTEIN, "The Return to Religion," *Proceedings, Central Conference of American Rabbis Year Book, 1952*.